STRETCHING MY MIND

STRETCHING MY MIND

EDWARD ALBEE

CARROLL & GRAF PUBLISHERS
NEW YORK

STRETCHING MY MIND

Carroll & Graf Publishers
An Imprint of Avalon Publishing Group Inc.
245 West 17th Street
11th Floor
New York, NY 10011

AVALON
publishing group incorporated

Portions of *Stretching My Mind* appeared in *Cosmopolitan, Nest, The New York Times, The New York Times Magazine, Playbill, Saturday Review, The Village Voice,* and *Zoetrope: All-Story*

"A Conversation with *Catch*" reprinted by permission of Knox College and *Catch* magazine.

" 'Instinctive Tingle' " appeared in *Edward Albee's Other Eye* (Hillwood Art Museum, 1990), reprinted by permission of the Hillwood Art Museum.

"Betty Parsons" conversation, conducted by Anne Cohen DePietro, is reprinted from *Shaping a Generation: The Art and Artists of Betty Parsons* (Huntington: Heckscher Museum of Art, 1999): 43-47. Reproduced by kind permission of Anne Cohen DePietro and the Heckscher Museum of Art.

"Context Is All" appeared in *From Idea to Matter: Nine Sculptors* (2000), reprinted by permission of Harry Rand.

"Interview with Steve Capra" appeared in *Theater Voices* (Scarecrow Press, 2004), reprinted by permission of the author and publisher.

"Borrowed Time" interview with Stephen Bottoms appeared in *The Cambridge Companion to Edward Albee* (Cambridge University Press, 2005), reprinted by permission of the author and publisher.

Library of Congress Cataloging-in-Publication Data is available.

ISBN-10: 0-78671-799-8
ISBN-13: 978-0-78671-799-6

Printed in the United States of America
Interior design by Maria Elias
Distributed by Publishers Group West

CONTENTS

FOREWORD

BY EDWARD ALBEE

A COLLECTION OF occasional pieces—meaning, as I understand it, pieces about occasions, *not* fripperies—can be a kind of high-wire act or, at best, a going out on several limbs.

Is it interesting what a playwright thinks about the visual arts (which so many of the pieces collected here deal with) or about music, or about critical journalism, or—indeed—his own craft? It *can* be if the playwright is knowledgeable about his subjects and has one or two provocative or illuminating ideas to throw out and if his essays are done to broaden his vision and to share a "professional" view of his surroundings, and not as dogma but as educated opinion.

Certainly I am not ashamed of the opinions I express here; nor do I claim revolutionary insights for them, but they may illuminate what goes through a playwright's mind as he reacts to stimulating experience in the areas akin to his creativity. Indeed, I tell my students that if they remain ignorant of or unreceptive to the visual arts and music they are hobbling their craft muscles, for a play is both seen and heard, and the ear and the eye must be highly developed for a playwright to use his craft to his full benefit.

I was fortunate in my education. While I was increasingly dismayed by my adoptive parents as I grew toward reason (my natural parents are unknown to me), by their dedicated anti-intellectualism and their profound racial and social prejudices,

I was fortunate that they had money and afforded me a splendid education, in private schools, where I was directed to the wonders of the arts while I was young enough to absorb these wonders without youngmanly prejudice.

And I am convinced that no one is fully educated without a full grounding in the arts.

So . . . Here we are. Forty-two pieces of my mind, written on commission, written as much as anything to inform me about what and how I was thinking. If they are useful beyond that . . . so much the better.

On *The Zoo Story*

1960

WITH THE EXCEPTION of a three-act sex farce I composed when I was twelve—the action of which occurred aboard an ocean liner, the characters of which were, for the most part, English gentry, and the title of which was, for some reason that escapes me now, *Aliqueen*—with the exception of that, *The Zoo Story* (1958), *The Death of Bessie Smith*, and *The Sandbox* (both 1959), are my first three plays.

The Zoo Story, written first, received production first—but not in the United States, where one might reasonably expect an American writer to get his first attention. *The Zoo Story* had its première in Berlin, Germany, on September 28, 1959. How it got to production so shortly after it was written, and how, especially, it got to Berlin, might be of interest—perhaps to point up the Unusual, the Unlikely, the Unexpected, which, with the exception of the fare the commercial theater setup spills out on its dogged audience each season, is the nature of the theater.

Shortly after *The Zoo Story* was completed, and while it was being read and politely refused by a number of New York producers (which was not to be unexpected, for no one at all had ever heard of its author, and it *was* a short play, and short plays *are,* unfortunately, anathema to producers and—supposedly—to audiences), a young composer friend of mine, William Flanagan by name, looked at the play, liked it, and sent it to several friends of his, among them David Diamond, another American composer, resident in Italy; Diamond liked the play and sent it on to a friend of *his,* a German actor, Pinkas Braun; Braun liked the play, translated it, made a tape recording of it, playing both its roles, which he sent on to Mrs. Stefani Hunzinger, who heads the drama department of the S. Fischer Verlag, a large publishing house in Frankfurt; she, in turn . . . well, through her it got to Berlin, and to production. From New York to Florence to Zurich to Frankfurt to Berlin. And finally back to New York where, on January 14, 1960, it received American production, off-Broadway, at the Provincetown Playhouse, on a double bill with Samuel Beckett's *Krapp's Last Tape.*

I went to Berlin for the opening of *The Zoo Story.* I had not planned to—it seemed like such a distance, such an expense—but enough friends said to me that, of course, I would be present at the first performance of my first play, that I found myself, quickly enough, replying, yes, yes, of course; I wouldn't miss it for the world. And so, I went; and I *wouldn't* have missed it for the world. I wouldn't have missed it for the world, despite the fact—as I have learned since—that, for this author, at least, opening nights do not really exist. They happen, but they take place as if in a dream: One concentrates, but one cannot see the stage action clearly; one can hear but barely; one tries to follow the play, but one can make no sense of it. And, if one is called to the stage afterwards to take a bow, one wonders why, for one can make no connection between the work just presented and one's self. Naturally, this feeling was complicated in the case of *The Zoo Story*, as the play was being presented in German, a language of which I knew not a word, and in Berlin, too, an awesome city. But, it has held true since. The high points of a person's life can be appreciated so often only in retrospect.

The Death of Bessie Smith also had its première in Berlin, while *The Sandbox* was done first in New York.

The Sandbox, which is fourteen minutes long, was written to satisfy a commission from the Festival of Two Worlds for a short dramatic piece for the Festival's summer program in Spoleto, Italy—where it was not performed. I was, at the time of the commission, at work on a rather longer play, *The American Dream*, which I subsequently put aside and have, at this writing, just taken up again. For *The Sandbox*, I extracted several of the characters from *The American Dream* and placed them in a situation different than, but related to, their predicament in the longer play. They seem happy out of doors, in *The Sandbox*, and I hope they will not be distressed back in a stuffy apartment, in *The American Dream*.

Along with *The American Dream*, I am at various stages of writing, or thinking about, three other plays: two other less-than-full-evening ones—*Bedlam* and *The Substitute Speaker* (this a working title)—and a full-evening play, *The Exorcism*, or: *Who's Afraid of Virginia Woolf?*

Careers are funny things. They begin mysteriously and, just as mysteriously, they can end; and I am at just the very beginning of what I hope will be a long and satisfying life in the theater. But, whatever happens, I am grateful to have had my novice work received so well, and so quickly.

Which Theater Is the Absurd One?

1962

A THEATER PERSON of my acquaintance—a man whose judgment must be respected, though more for the infallibility of his intuition than for his reasoning—remarked just the other week, "The Theater of the Absurd has had it; it's on its way out; it's through."

Now this, on the surface of it, seems to be a pretty funny attitude to be taking toward a theater movement which has, only in the past couple of years, been impressing itself on the American public consciousness. Or is it? Must we judge that a theater of such plays as Samuel Beckett's *Krapp's Last Tape*, Jean Genet's *The Balcony* (both long, long runners off-Broadway), and Eugène Ionesco's *Rhinoceros*—which, albeit in a hoked-up production, had a substantial season on Broadway—has been judged by the theater public and found wanting?

And shall we have to assume that the Theater of the Absurd Repertory Company, currently playing at New York's off-Broadway Cherry Lane Theater—presenting works by Beckett, Ionesco, Genet, Arrabal, Jack Richardson, Kenneth Koch, and myself—being the first such collective representation of the movement in the United States, is also a kind of farewell to the movement? For that matter, just what *is* the Theater of the Absurd?

Well, let me come at it obliquely. When I was told, about a year ago, that I was considered a member in good standing of the Theater of the Absurd I was deeply offended. I was deeply offended because I had never heard the term before and I immediately assumed that it applied to the theater uptown—Broadway.

What (I was reasoning to myself) could be more absurd than a theater in which the aesthetic criterion is something like this: A "good" play is one which makes money; a "bad" play (in the sense of "Naughty! Naughty!" I guess) is one which does not; a theater in which performers have plays rewritten to correspond to the public relations image of themselves; a theater in which playwrights are encouraged (what a funny word!) to think of themselves as little cogs in a great big wheel; a theater in which imitation has given way to imitation of imitation; a theater in which London "hits" are, willy-nilly, in a kind of reverse of chauvinism, greeted in a manner not unlike a colony's obeisance to the Crown; a theater in which real estate owners and theater party managements predetermine the success of unknown quantities; a theater in which everybody scratches and bites for billing as though it meant access to the last bomb shelter on earth; a theater in which, in a given season, there was not a single performance of a play by Beckett, Brecht, Chekhov, Genet, Ibsen, O'Casey, Pirandello, Shaw, Strindberg—or Shakespeare? What, indeed, I thought, could be more absurd than that? (My conclusions . . . obviously.)

For it emerged that the Theater of the Absurd, aside from being the title of an excellent book by Martin Esslin on what is loosely called the avant-garde theater, was a somewhat less than fortunate catch-all phrase to describe the philosophical attitudes and theater methods of a number of Europe's finest and most adventurous playwrights and their followers.

I was less offended, but still a little dubious. Simply: I don't like labels; they can be facile and can lead to nonthink on the part of the public. And unless it is understood that the playwrights of the Theater of the Absurd represent a group only in the sense that they seem to be doing something of the same thing in vaguely similar ways at approximately the same time—unless this is understood, then the labeling itself will be more absurd than the label.

Playwrights, by nature, are grouchy, withdrawn, envious, greedy, suspicious and, in general, quite nice people—and the majority of them wouldn't be caught dead in a colloquy remotely resembling the following:

Ionesco: *(At a Left Bank café table, spying Beckett and Genet strolling past in animated conversation)* Hey! Sam! Jean!

Genet: Hey, it's Eugene! Sam, it's Eugene!

Beckett: Well, I'll be damned. Hi there, Eugene boy.

Ionesco: Sit down, kids.

Genet: Sure thing.

Ionesco: *(Rubbing his hands together)* Well, what's new in the Theater of the Absurd?

Beckett: Oh, less than a lot of people think. *(They all laugh.)*

Etc. No. Not very likely. Get a playwright alone sometime, get a few drinks in him, and maybe he'll be persuaded to sound off about his "intention" and the like—and hate himself for it the next day. But put a group of playwrights together in a room, and the conversation—if there is any—will, more likely than not, concern itself with sex, restaurants, and the movies.

Very briefly, then—and reluctantly, because I am a playwright and would much rather talk about sex, restaurants, and the movies—and stumblingly, because I do not pretend to understand it entirely, I will try to define the Theater of the Absurd. As I get it, the Theater of the Absurd is an absorption-in-art of certain existentialist and postexistentialist philosophical concepts having to do, in the main, with man's attempts to make sense for himself out of his senseless position in a world which makes no sense—which makes no sense because the moral, religious, political and social structures man has erected to "illusion" himself have collapsed.

Albert Camus put it this way: "A world that can be explained by reasoning, however faulty, is a familiar world. But in a universe that is suddenly deprived of illusions and of light, man feels a stranger. His is an irremediable exile, because he is deprived of memories of a lost homeland as much as he lacks the hope of a promised land to come. This divorce between man and his life, the actor and his setting, truly constitutes the feeling of Absurdity."

And Eugene Ionesco says this: "Absurd is that which is devoid of purpose . . . Cut off from his religious, metaphysical, and transcendental roots, man is lost; all his actions become senseless, absurd, useless."

*   *   *

And to sum up the movement, Martin Esslin writes, in his book *The Theater of the Absurd*: "Ultimately, a phenomenon like the Theater of the Absurd does not reflect despair or a return to dark irrational forces but expresses modern man's endeavor to come to terms with the world in which he lives. It attempts to make him face up to the human condition as it really is, to free him from illusions that are bound to cause constant maladjustment and disappointment . . . For the dignity of man lies in his ability to face reality in all its senselessness; to accept it freely, without fear, without illusions—and to laugh at it."

Amen.

(And while we're on the subject of Amen, one wearies of the complaint that the Theater of the Absurd playwrights alone are having at God these days. The notion that God is dead, indifferent, or insane—a notion blasphemous, premature, or academic depending on your persuasion—while surely a tenet of some of the playwrights under discussion, is, it seems to me, of a piece with Mr. Tennessee Williams's description of the Deity, in *The Night of the Iguana,* as "a senile delinquent.")

So much for the attempt to define terms. Now, what of this theater? What of this theater in which, for example, a legless old couple live out their lives in twin ashcans, surfacing occasionally for food or conversation (Samuel Beckett's *Endgame*); in which a man is seduced, and rather easily, by a girl with three well-formed and functioning noses (Eugene Ionesco's *Jack, or The Submission*); in which, on the same stage, one group of black actors is playing at pretending to be white and another group of black actors is playing at pretending to be black (Jean Genet's *The Blacks*)?

* * *

What of this theater? Is it, as it has been accused of being, obscure, sordid, destructive, antitheater, perverse, and absurd (in the sense of foolish)? Or is it merely, as I have so often heard it put, that, "This sort of stuff is too depressing, too . . . too mixed-up; I go to the theater to relax and have a good time."

I would submit that it is this latter attitude—that the theater is a place to relax and have a good time—in conflict with the purpose of the Theater of the Absurd—which is to make a man face up to the human condition as it really is—that has produced all the brouhaha and the dissent. I would submit that the Theater of the Absurd, in the sense that it is truly the contemporary theater, facing as it does man's condition as it is, is the Realistic theater of our time; and that the supposed Realistic theater—the term used here to mean most of what is done on Broadway—in the sense that it panders to the public need for self-congratulation and reassurance and presents a false picture of ourselves to ourselves is, with an occasional very lovely exception, really truly the Theater of the Absurd.

And I would submit further that the health of a nation, a society, can be determined by the art it demands. We have insisted of television and our movies that they not have anything to do with anything, that they be our never-never land; and if we demand this same function of our live theater, what will be left of the visual-auditory arts—save the dance (in which nobody talks) and music (to which nobody listens)?

It has been my fortune, the past two or three years, to travel around a good deal, in pursuit of my career—Berlin, London, Buenos Aires, for example; and I have discovered a couple of interesting things. I have discovered that audiences in these and other major cities demand of their commercial theater—and get— a season of plays in which the froth and junk are the exception and not the rule. To take a case: in Berlin, in 1959, Adamov, Genet, Beckett, and Brecht (naturally) were playing the big houses; this past fall, Beckett again, Genet again, Pinter twice, etc. To take another case: in Buenos Aires there are over a hundred experimental theaters.

These plays cannot be put on in Berlin over the head of a protesting or an indifferent audience; these experimental theaters cannot exist in Buenos Aires without subscription. In the end—and it must always come down to this, no matter what other failings a theater may have—in the end a public will get what it deserves, and no better.

I have also discovered, in my wanderings, that young people throng to what is new and fresh in the theater. Happily, this holds true in the United States as well. At the various colleges I have gone to to speak I have found an eager, friendly, and knowledge-able audience, an audience which is as dismayed by the Broadway scene as any proselytizer for the avant-garde. I have found among young people an audience which is not so preconditioned by pap as to have cut off half of its responses. (It is interesting to note, by the way, that if an off-Broadway play has a substantial run, its audiences will begin young and grow older as the run goes on, cloth coats give way to furs, walkers and subway riders to taxi-takers. Exactly the opposite is true on Broadway.)

The young, of course, are always questioning values, knocking the status quo about, considering shibboleths to see if they are pronounceable. In time, it is to be regretted, most of them—the kids—will settle down to their own version of the easy, the stan-dard; but in the meanwhile . . . in the meanwhile they are a wonderful, alert, alive, accepting audience.

And I would go so far as to say that it is the responsibility of everyone who pretends any interest at all in the theater to get up off their overly-priced seats and find out what the theater is *really* about. For it is a lazy public which produces a slothful and irresponsible theater.

Now, I would suspect that my theater friend with the infallible intuition is probably right when he suggests that the Theater of the Absurd (or the avant-garde theater, or whatever you want to call it) as it now stands is on its way out. Or at least is undergoing change. All living organisms undergo constant change. And while it is certain that the nature of this theater will remain constant, its forms, its methods—its devices, if you will—most necessarily will undergo mutation.

This theater has no intention of running downhill; and the younger playwrights will make use of the immediate past and mould it to their own needs. (Harold Pinter, for example, could not have written *The Caretaker* had Samuel Beckett not existed, but Pinter is, nonetheless, moving in his own direction.) And it is my guess that the theater in the United States will always hew more closely to the post–Ibsen/Chekhov tradition than does the theater in France, let us say. It is our nature as a country, a society. But we will experiment, and we will expect your attention.

For just as it is true that our response to color and form was forever altered once the impressionist painters put their minds to canvas, it is just as true that the playwrights of the Theater of the Absurd have forever altered our response to the theater.

And one more point: The avant-garde theater is fun; it is free-swinging, bold, iconoclastic, and often wildly, wildly funny. If you will approach it with childlike innocence—putting your standard responses aside, for they do not apply—if you will approach it on its own terms, I think you will be in for a liberating surprise. I think you may no longer be content with plays that you can't remember halfway down the block. You will not only be doing yourself some good, but you will be having a great time, to boot. And even though it occurs to me that such a fine combination must be sinful, I still recommend it.

SOME NOTES ON NONCONFORMITY

1962

HERE IS A list of people and things: Michelangelo Antonioni, John Cage, Jules Pfeiffer, Norman Mailer, Henry Miller, *The Apple, Brecht on Brecht, The Village Voice,* and whatever book on conformity has come out the past week.

It isn't a bad list, but I propose to attack it. I propose to attack it because it is the sort of list the middle-brow taste-makers dish out to the middle-brow tasters almost every time you turn around.

Almost invariably, when I brush up against a bunch of people who are reasonably well educated, mildly "liberal," nonindigent, carelessly well dressed, and casually well spoken, I can count on hearing names like the above lead from the conversation like so much wet from a sponge.

And while these names—Cage, Mailer, and group—are, for the most part, fine—I mean, they're all either avant-garde or far-out, or something—one worries. One worries because, while everybody these days is nonconformist, or pretends to be (conformity has become a dirty word), the list-makers are poking around the Arts Pudding and scooping out whatever plums happen to be floating on the surface—with the result that we end up with list after list of the *fashionable* nonconformist people and things, the acceptable iconoclasts, the not-so-far-from-center far-outs.

One must always mistrust fashion, because it is, as often as not, arbitrary; and the assumption that one can become informed of, and participate in, the intellectual temper of our time through reliance on any breathlessly composed list of fashionable far-outs is funny and sad—and, what is much worse, terribly conformist.

Now, with no desire to denigrate the qualities of any of the—however unwittingly—above-listed, I ask you to consider the following: Antonioni is a fine director, but one had best know Bunuel and Eisenstein, too; Cage may be a fine composer, but after the silences and radio concerts, for *real* kicks try some truly far-outs like G. De Machaut, V. Thomson, and O. Berio; Norman Mailer and Henry Miller both have something to say, but a really full diet will include Jane Austen and John Rechy, Turgenev and William Burroughs; *Brecht on Brecht* is a nice kindergarten introduction to the man's work, but don't pretend you know Brecht by it; *The Village Voice* is okay I suppose, in its self-consciously virile way (though I do with they'd write in English), but if you want to see what a really first-class liberal intellectualist sheet looks like, you might investigate the *New Statesman*.

And so on.

The tyrannies are everywhere, and it is a shame to see people paying mere lip service to an idea—putting on shelves, or quick-reference mental file cards for instant dropping, what they should be putting into their minds. Our talented people are improperly used if they become possessions; you must not possess them—you must let them possess you. You must not invite them into your world—you must enter theirs, be taken, and move deeper.

BROADWAY EXCESSES

1962

SEVERAL SUNDAYS AGO, on the front page of the entertainment section of this newspaper, there appeared a troika of photographs—of, reading from stage-right to stage-left, Jack Richardson, myself, and Rick Besoyan. We were, each of us, in Shubert Alley, and we were, each of us, hovering near a billboard for *Night of the Iguana* or *A Man for All Seasons* or something.

The point of it all was, it appears, that here were three off-Broadway playwrights—playwrights who had made something of a reputation for themselves off-Broadway (Jack Richardson for *The Prodigal* and *Gallows Humor*, Rick Besoyan for *Little Mary Sunshine*, and me for *The Zoo Story*, *The American Dream*, etc.)—who were, now, all of a sudden, in the same season, going to have works of theirs done on Broadway—Jack Richardson with *Lorenzo*, Rick Besoyan with *Student Gypsy or Prince of Liederkranz*, and me with *Who's Afraid of Virginia Woolf?*

* * *

It all looked all right to me—certainly no sillier than any other spread I've appeared in, in various combinations with Jack Gelber or Arthur Kopit or Jack Richardson or Rick Besoyan, and we have appeared in some pretty bizarre groupings, not the least of which was in a ladies' magazine last spring, where the bunch of us, with Arnold Weinstein added, was photographed peering out of a huge packing case, rather as if we were about to be shipped somewhere.

In fact, we have been photographed together, or similarly, so much that whenever we meet for the newest layout as often as not we chance some not very droll fripperies about the Marx Brothers in *A Night Off Broadway,* or something like that. We do not mean to be churlish, but we do brood, occasionally, on the interchange-ability of our identities.

And, it would seem, a number of people have been brooding on the trio layout in this paper several Sundays ago. Ten or twelve persons have brooded out loud to me—and while I don't know if Jack Richardson and Rick Besoyan have been brooded at in a like way, the broodings I've heard are of a voice, and go something like this: "Well, I see you off-Broadway tots are finally putting on long pants, hunh? I mean, that's the way it looks, by gum—yer pitchers up there on the front page, and all. Boy, you all sure didn't have that sort of stuff when you had yer things done off-Broadway. Wow, the way you all thought you had careers goin', it must've given you quite a chill to find out you didn't matter until this season."

Well, I'm sure the *New York Times* doesn't give a hoot what my attitude is toward this interpretation of their attitude, and cer-tainly cares less about what my attitude is toward their attitude toward this interpretation of their attitude. And besides, the *New*

York Times was, if I am not mistaken, off-Broadway's first steadfast daily newspaper friend, so I will not presume to defend the *Times*.

Unlikely Philistinism and more likely overprotective Off-Broadwayism to the side, it is interesting that there is, no matter how many ways a lot of us would like to slice it, even at this late date a large body of opinion which holds that the theater world is flat, that Broadway is the center of the universe, and that if one were to take a cab below Fourteenth Street one would find no worthwhile theater—only an abyss. Sane men know this is not so.

Everybody knows that off-Broadway, in one season, puts on more fine plays than Broadway does in any five seasons. Everybody knows that Beckett, Genet, and Brecht (to take three Europeans, and keep chauvinism's head under water) are more important playwrights than almost anybody writing on Broadway today. Everybody knows this; everybody knows everything; yet award time, for example (yes, and reward time, too), finds the world suddenly pre-Copernican.

I wonder about all this, and wonder about it now, especially, since *Who's Afraid of Virginia Woolf?*—the fifth play I have written—is about to open on Broadway (the other four having been berthed off-Broadway), and Broadway is a land whose currency and customs regulations I do not wholly understand.

I know, for example, that this play is going to be the "big test" for me, but I don't know exactly why. I do know that the Billy Rose Theater (which is a nice theater) is six times as large as the Provincetown Playhouse (which is a nice theater). I do know that *Who's Afraid of Virginia Woolf?* is costing a lot more to mount than *The Zoo Story,* say; but since the double bill of *Krapp's Last Tape* and *The Zoo Story* cost about $10 to put on, that is sort of inevitable. I do know that *Woolf*—as I heard somebody call it recently—is in the hands of a brilliant cast and director; but I've already seen plays of mine done in a fashion that makes me happy I stumbled into the theater in the first place.

I do know that, uptown, "success" is so often equated with cash; while, downtown, value does not always have a dollar sign attached. I do know that the national publicity salvos following a Broadway success are deafening compared to the burp gun reports attending something fine off-Broadway; but I also know that all these noises are more concerned with the images of things than with the things themselves. And I know that there is an ugly amount of money to be made on Broadway—but, then again, there is an ugly amount of money to be made off-Broadway, too.

I know all these things, but none of them answers my question. Could it be that it has nothing to do with logistics at all, but is simply a matter of the fact that *Who's Afraid of Virginia Woolf?* is my first so-called "full-length" play? I doubt that, because it is longer than conventional "full-length," while the others were shorter. And we know that in a responsible press there is no double standard of judgment, that a play is a play and must be so judged, be it produced in a vacant lot or in Buckingham Palace. (Well, there is a slight double standard, in the sense that off-Broadway plays are often praised in spite of their production, while uptown the reverse is sometimes true. But, all in all, things are fair.)

Still, the question nags. Now, naturally, I hope that *Who's Afraid of Virginia Woolf?* is a good play—if I were not convinced that it had some merit I would not let it be produced. (And there's nothing quite like an objective viewpoint, is there, Edward?) Nonetheless, I am told by some of the cognoscenti that if this play is a success it will be a more important success than the others, and that if it is a failure the failure will be more disastrous than it could be downtown. It may be so, but I can't quite get it through my head why.

But, no matter. It is idle speculations like these that might just as well as not occupy any mind a week before opening. After all, the play is written, and it is in the best of possible hands.

And as for the rest . . . well, we shall see.

CARSON McCULLERS

1963

CARSON MCCULLERS IS indeed a curious magician.

Examine this: she is a lady who, at an age when most girls have nothing more on their minds than their next cotillion, can conjure a work like *The Ballad of the Sad Café*—a work of great wisdom—and then leave it lay in a drawer for years, on the assumption that no one needed it.

Examine this: she is a lady who, as a girl, trained as a concert pianist until she discovered that the keyboard of the typewriter, when played with magic, produced a music wilder and more beautiful than any other instrument.

Examine this: in the caldron of her work there is the stuff for every literary prize—and yet the prizes elude her, as they do most witches and warlocks. Oh, pity the prizes!

Examine this: she is both Child and Sage; Pain and Joy. She has mastered the card tricks of both art and life, and she has seen equally clearly the sleight of hand of reality and the truth which resides in legerdemain.

She is kind enough to call me her friend.

LILLIAN ROSS

1963

BEFORE THE PUBLICATION of *Vertical and Horizontal*, her first extended fiction, Lillian Ross had made her reputation primarily as a *reporter*—as the author of three books of nonfiction, two of which, *Portrait of Hemingway* and *Picture*, gained for her a reputation both enviable and nonenviable. She was hailed as a reporter of brilliant perception and objectivity, a real no-nonsense girl; at the same time her objectivity was called, by some, the kind of "objectivity" which could, in its cold, beady-eyed, exactly-factual-and-therefore-unfair-and-distorting way, make anyone look like a fool.

Certainly, in *Portrait of Hemingway*—a record of a couple of days during which Miss Ross tagged along with the great man as he Hemingwayed himself around New York City during a brief visit—the author of *A Farewell to Arms* enters the book as something of a sacred cow and leaves it with the word "sacred" scratched out.

* * *

And in *Picture*—a record of the simultaneous creation and destruction of the movie *The Red Badge of Courage*—Dore Schary is dealt a crippling blow to the belly, and the patina on the image of John Huston is scraped off to show a considerably baser metal underneath.

(In her third book of reporting, *The Player*, with photographs by her sister, Helen, Lillian Ross permits a large group of actors and actresses to run on, unbridled, about their favorite subject—themselves. The effect is precisely what you might imagine: numbing.)

There is no question that Lillian Ross treats her real-life subjects without reverence for the image of themselves they would prefer to display to the public—or to themselves, for that matter. But to the attack that she approaches her victims with relish and without pity, I would answer that she has no victims, merely subjects; that she approaches her subjects not without pity but without piety.

And now Miss Ross has published her first book of fiction, a collection of related stories called *Vertical and Horizontal*. The book has its faults, but they are minor; it is, in the main, a superb work.

Faults first. Two stories in the book—chapters three and seven (there are ten)—hardly belong. They both have nice writing and both concern subsidiary characters, but they are unnecessary resting places, and one wonders if they were included for any reason more persuasive than that they existed. And, in a couple of other stories, there are sentences of exposition and character definition which would be pertinent were the stories to stand alone but which, in context of the collection, are redundant.

(And there are, in the first edition at least, a couple of typos, but one doubts that they should be charged to Miss Ross.)

So much for the faults. They are, to repeat, minor. The successes are major.

Vertical and Horizontal has, for a 223-page book, an extraordinary number of characters: over forty have speaking parts, and another twenty or so are referred to. What is remarkable is Miss Ross's way of giving this company, whether by full canvas or by single line of the brush, full substance and breath. They—all of them—become as real as Schary or Huston or Hemingway— realer, perhaps, because they are fictions and more credible. Miss Ross creates, and then observes her creations, with precision, brevity, and depth. It is a virtue.

One could say that there are two major characters in the book—Dr. Spencer Fifield, a still-fairly-young, unmarried M.D., and Dr. Al Blauberman, his analyst. Both men are near-monsters. They are hollow men; they are insensitive, small, mean, are amoral; they are climbers, these men, and it is their effect on each other, and on the people whose lives touch theirs, that is the core of the book.

Spencer Fifield cannot "feel anything"; he does not have "give-love." He had, as Miss Ross puts it, "soaked up a multitude of ideas about feelings. There wasn't a human feeling that he hadn't learned to label or interpret or explain—especially other people's feelings. But what, or where, were his own? He had never found out. Spencer did not know what love was. His friends and his analyst were able to give him rules, regulations, definitions, directions, admonitions, boos, and cheers, and Spencer memorized them, all very carefully, but it did not bring him any closer to the thing itself."

Spencer Fifield knows he should have emotional involvements, but when he propositions a girl he will say, "Let's go to bed; I should have an emotional involvement."

Spencer Fifield longs to "belong," but the only people to whom he can really relate are his sickest patients—the crippled, the dying.

Spencer Fifield feels empty because he is empty; he feels inferior because he is.

Dr. Al Blauberman, Spencer's analyst, was himself an M.D. who moved into his present profession because there was more money in it, because his working hours would be set, because there was more status to it, because it would give him a sense of power (of existing).

Dr. Blauberman almost succeeds in destroying one of his patients, a young, easygoing musician who went into analysis with Blauberman because his doctor, Spencer Fifield, urged him to because the young man does not covet power and money (things Blauberman knows to be the goals) and has a good, healthy relationship with his father (Blauberman hates and has disowned his own father because he was poor).

Dr. Blauberman despises and envies most of his fellow analysts, especially those more successful than he and those damn "refugees."

Dr. Blauberman has had Spencer Fifield as a patient for a number of years, and promises standards, by the standards of both of them, in adjusting Spencer Fifield to society. By the end of the book, Spencer Fifield has been removed from the outerspace vacuum of his isolation and plunged into, drowned in an environment whose values are superficial, self-deluding, and materialistic enough to accommodate a man of Spencer's qualities.

It is a happy ending. It is brilliant.

It is—the whole book—also a number of other things. It is an attack on the school of analysts who would adjust a man to his society without first relating him to himself. It is a terrifying examination of the living death, the pseudo-involved cliché-ridden mindless living death that passes for existing in our vast middle-class society. It is also a very funny book.

Oh, most of the humor is dark and sad and deeply troubling, and forces one to view horror and absurdity and futility with the double sight of great laughter and great pity, but a lot of it is just plain funny even while the wit is always more than a little acerbic.

But the most astonishing thing about *Vertical and Horizontal*, and the most extraordinary of Lillian Ross's enormous gifts, is that we care. Spencer Fifield is, for lack of a better word, the hero of the book, and we truly care about this man, about this hollow, hopeless man, and we care because Miss Ross makes us see that he is helpless—that monster is victim, that the hopeless man cries out hopelessly, that the emptiness can never be filled, only circumscribed, that the most miserable of men, the man who knows he suffers but cannot grasp his suffering, cannot feel it, is not any less a human being, only a much sadder one.

It is Miss Ross's compassion that surfaces. Without it, the book would be cold, cruel, and distasteful. With it, the book is a triumph.

AD LIBS ON THEATER

1965

ON DIRECTORS

From the playwright's point of view, the function of the director is to take what the author has put down on a page—the absolute and total reality that exists on the page—to watch it through its disintegration into the hands of actors. A play starts as a total reality, and when it goes into a rehearsal situation it completely disintegrates into artificiality. It has to. The responsibility of the director is to bring the play intact, from its first reality, to the first moment of rehearsal back to the time when the play reaches an audience intact with the original reality and the original intention of the author.

The director must speak *for* the author, must speak *to* the actors in a very special way—in a way that will accomplish the author's intention in terms that perhaps are very far from the author's intention. The emergence of the first reality can be gotten by so many indirections, which will vary with the gifts and methods of the director.

It has been said that the American stage is a director's theater because plays are changed so much from their original script by the time they reach an audience, and that implicit in that is that the directors do the majority of the changing. It is within the author's contract not to allow changes in a script. If an author gives up his authority to a director in script changes, to actors, to producers, to backers, that's in dereliction to his own responsibility to himself. I would imagine that directors can make it a director's theater only if they do (1) the work of dead playwrights, or (2) the work of playwrights who are so weak or such bad writers that they can't keep it their own theater.

ON THE AUDIENCE

When will we return the theater to the audience? Well, I don't think we should, frankly. Does the tree that falls in the forest, nobody hearing it, make any sound? I've always thought that it did. The theater may well be the possession of the audience but the playwright is not. The play is not. When I was in the Soviet Union last winter, I had a number of arguments with aestheticians, theater directors, and playwrights. All of them seemed to have the feeling that the primary responsibility in the theater is the playwright's responsibility to the audience and to the glorification of the society in which he lives. I tried to point out that in the United States, and in most of Western Europe, most creative writing is in some way critical of the society in which it occurs. Naturally, I had a number of arguments about this attitude in the Soviet Union.

But a play is the possession of the man who wrote it. It's his responsibility to communicate. But it's his responsibility to communicate the ideas that he wishes, be they popular or unpopular.

It's the responsibility of the audience to go to a theater in open-minded fashion to accept what the author says in a free way, not to go with preconceptions, not to go demanding a certain kind of theater. There has to be a give-and-take in the theater, and it mustn't always be the author expected to pander to an audience. At the same time I'm not trying to suggest that the playwright should consider himself part of any fascist elite. He shouldn't write above his audience. By writing above his audience he's writing above himself because most playwrights are their favorite audience, their most enthusiastic audience and sometimes, they feel, their most perceptive audience.

But the whole concept of the theater belonging to the audience to determine what should be written and what playwrights should say—and which is a thing, by the way, which is beginning to infect more and more of our daily criticism of theater and of all the arts—is a criminal act.

ON CRITICS

In the theater an author has got to be grateful, quite often, for good reviews for the wrong reason. It's enormously fortunate that an author can receive good reviews for exactly the reason that he intended, for the reason that he wrote a play. I found with *Who's Afraid of Virginia Woolf?*, for example, that if I put together the comments of ten or twelve critics, as long as the comments weren't contradictory, and a number of them were, I could come up with a reasonably good approximation of what, after the fact, I decided I wanted to tell people that the play was about. I find usually with critics that I take from their reviews what makes me seem a great deal more organized and intelligent than I am and pretend that was my intention.

I've been rather annoyed by the enormous overattention that some critics paid to the symbolism in *Tiny Alice*—the allegory search, the symbol hunting. The play was written out of a certain conviction, about what I am not sure, but written with a certain emotional and perhaps intellectual intensity. It was my intention that the audience would experience the play without playing all the games of allegory searching and symbol hunting. I do have the, perhaps paranoid, feeling that a lot of the encouragements the critics have given the audience—the future audiences on how to hunt the snark—had to do with some of their own confusion, or perhaps unwillingness to allow the not entirely comfortable emotional aspects of the play to take over. But any play that's halfway decent has got to be an emotional experience first, unless it's a totally didactic play. If you're writing about characters—and I assumed I was, rather than about symbols—and that I was writing about action rather than about allegory—then the experience is the important thing and then allegory might occur in the mind afterward.

ON CHARACTERS

So many people are always asking, "Mr. Albee, why are all the women in your plays terrible?" They're not. I found the character of Martha in *Who's Afraid of Virginia Woolf?*, for example, one of the most complete female women that I had experienced in the theater in a long time. I found her quite worthy of sympathy, affection even and love. In *Tiny Alice,* the character of Miss Alice, performing rather unpleasant tasks as is her assignment, is not an unsympathetic character as far as I am concerned.

In *The American Dream,* which is, I suppose, sort of an attack on a number of our mores, the character of Grandma certainly is an enormously sympathetic character, worthy of a good deal of affection and love.

The dramatist is always commenting on people, and the problem is to comment effectively and make art out of it. You're making a critical comment when you create the life of somebody. You can only make propaganda out of it if you think somebody is entirely bad, entirely good. You must expose both attributes. A character totally unworthy of sympathy or love would be totally unworthy of attention—the author's attention or the audience's.

ON DISCOVERY

When I was writing *Tiny Alice,* to a certain extent I didn't have any idea what I was doing. When I write plays, the writing of the play is an act of discovery for me. I find out what I have been thinking about. I find out what's bothering me. And a certain time after the play I can say to myself, "Ha! That is what I intended." That's why I was half sporting about taking things from the critics.

I recently discovered that when Edward Albee writes a play about ideas he confuses more people than he intended, which may suggest that Mr. Albee, when he writes about ideas, is rather confused himself.

I also discovered that audiences are not necessarily put off by being confused. I've learned once again that indifference is the worst thing, though I didn't write the play to confuse or arouse controversy. I find it encouraging that audiences care enough about the experience of the play to involve themselves in it.

Noël Coward

1965

QUITE A FEW years ago—just before the Second World War, or maybe not—a poll was taken to find out who was the most famous person in the world. I have no idea how this was gone about, if it was, and with what degree of thoroughness, but the results were published—unless I dreamed it all, though I don't think I did—and the most famous person in the world was found to be Charlie Chaplin. I remember being surprised, having thought that it would have been Christ, perhaps, or Hitler. But then I thought about it, and realized that in spite of their considerable impact on what we choose to call our civilization, both Christ and Hitler (and I don't enjoy having the two of them in the same sentence any more than you do) had, in a worldwide context, a relatively localized influence. I realized that if the poll were on the level there would have been millions of people, in Asia and Africa, for example, whose brush with either the Christ or the Antichrist would have been minimal, and that these millions of people might much more likely have seen the funny man with the cane and the big shoes.

I doubt that Noël Coward made the top twenty on the world-wide list, but I would be surprised if his name did not figure high—at least in the European and North American tables. I have met people, to take a case or two, who could not place E. M. Forster, or Arnold Schönberg, or Brancusi, but I have never met anyone who said, "Who is Noël Coward?" Indeed, if you have written a number of famous plays, composed a clutch of songs which have become embedded in the standard repertory, written and directed well-known films, and acted, to acclaim, for years and years, who in hell is *not* going to know who you are?

Consider my astonishment, then, over the following telephone exchange between the publishers of *Three Plays by Noël Coward* and myself.

"Mr. Albee, we wonder if you'd like to do the introduction to a collection of Noël Coward's plays we're planning."

(Brief pause on my side, not caused by my wondering if I'd like to, but only if I had the time, since I was working on a play of my own.)

"Mr. Albee?"

"Oh! Yes, I'd love to. How did you know I like his plays so much? Let's see now, I'll just have to read them over again . . . you know, to . . ."

"Well, we'll try to find you copies."

"What do you mean *find*?"

"Find. They're all out of print."

"You're kidding."

No, they were not kidding. Through some kind of negligence, Noël Coward's plays had been allowed to fall out of print in the United States. Happily, three of them are back again, in this collection.

Read them again, and if for some reason—like you're so young you've learned to read only this year, or you've been locked up without books since the twenties—you've never read them, try it. You're in for quite a treat.

Wait. "Treat" is not the word I'm after, though it is valid. "Experience" is better. You're in for quite an experience. I don't know if you will become slave to all three printed here (I am still very much subject to two of them), but you will, without question, be reminded of the three qualities possessed by all plays of any matter—literary excellence (by which I mean rhythm and sound), dramatic sure-footedness and pertinence.

Mr. Coward writes dialogue as well as any man going; it is seemingly effortless, surprising in the most wonderfully surprising places, and "true"—very, very true. He is, as well, a dramatic mountain goat; his plays are better made than most—but not in the sense of the superimposed paste job of form, but from within: order more than form. And Mr. Coward's subjects—the ways we kid ourselves that we do not exist with each other and with ourselves—have not, unless my mind has been turned inward too long, gone out of date.

Notwithstanding it all, Noël Coward can be a bore. He bores his admirers every time he gets within earshot of a reporter by announcing how old-fashioned a writer he is, how the theater has left him behind, how he does not understand the—to use an expression vague and confusing enough to have become meaning-less and therefore dangerous—"avant garde" playwrights of today, feels no sympathy with them.

It is difficult to imagine him wringing his hands and seeking reassurance when he says these things, and it is equally difficult to think that there is a smug tone to the voice, so I don't really know what Mr. Coward's problem is. Whatever it may be, let me remind him that the theater goes in many directions simultaneously, and that plays like *The Adding Machine* or Georg Kaiser's *Gas*—both terribly "avant garde" for their day—are as musty now as anything by Scribe, while Gogol, say, has the laugh on everybody. Let me add that both Samuel Beckett and Harold Pinter—to grab an "avant garde" father-and-son combo out of the hat (also, hopefully, to choose two playwrights Mr. Coward is out of sorts about)—have, as their subjects, his own preoccupations, have, as well, a precisely honed sense of form and sound. Let me remind Mr. Coward further that what becomes old-fashioned has within it, from the start, the dry rot to permit the disintegration, that the fungus of public fashion, on the other hand, is superficial. To finish this point up, let me shoot out a question: What is the difference between a passacaglia written in a tone-row system and one composed tonally—save method, the stylistic point of departure?

But let me stop being churlish. A man I know and like and whose opinion I respect, a man involved with the theater, a man who has produced the work of such playwrights as Beckett, Ionesco, Pinter, Arrabal and Ugo Betti, said to me not long ago that he greatly admired Noël Coward's plays, that he thought Coward a better playwright than Bernard Shaw and that Coward's plays would be on the boards long after most of the men writing today had been forgotten.

Now, I don't much like to make public judgments about other playwrights, for when I do I hear myself saying harsh things about Ibsen, for example, or boring people with my joy at seeing Brecht done correctly twice in my life. That is why I have put down what my producer friend said. I will only nod and say that this book contains some very fine playwriting, and that Noël Coward should relax about his work; it stands a very good chance of being with us for a long, long time.

JAMES PURDY

1966

I WONDER WHAT the state of American letters would be if our writers did not insist on expatriating themselves. For every Flannery O'Connor who stayed put in the South, there are a dozen like Carson McCullers and Tennessee Williams who have left home in order to see home. Most of our writers are from some place far distant from where we find them working.

For example: there is, right now, living in Brooklyn—deep in Brooklyn—a wonderfully cheerful, softspoken man who, unlike most writers, wears a hat when he goes out, and whose telephone is almost always either busy or disconnected. His name is James Purdy, and he is widely reputed to be one of our few fine seriocomic novelists. His accent tells us he is not from the East. (He is, in fact, from Ohio.)

I have no idea why Purdy left home but, then again, I'm not certain I know exactly why Hemingway left home, or Steinbeck, or all of the others who found they should, unless it is simply, as one writer put it, that "You have to go a long distance out of your way to come back a short distance correctly."

The fact is enough: most of our serious writers have put down roots far from their homes, are pioneers of sorts.

And who, exactly, is James Purdy—this cheerful man from somewhere else who has set his hat down deep in Brooklyn? Among those who know his work, the opinion is violent and various. The late Dame Edith Sitwell—a lady whose opinions were strong and more often than not unfavorable—called him probably the finest American writer in the past hundred years. More recently, a critic whose name I don't recall at the moment but whose style was awful, insisted that Purdy can't even write a correct sentence. And there are readers who will praise one or two of his books and damn the others—though I have seldom found any two readers praising and damning the same books. The books include *The Nephew, The Color of Darkness, Cabot Wright Begins, Children Is All,* and *Malcolm.*

This last, *Malcolm,* is my present concern, for I have adapted it to the stage. The moment of commercial truth for the play will be this Tuesday, when it officially opens at the Shubert Theater.

I shall most certainly not try to explain "Malcolm" before the press is in, nor do I think I shall need to afterward. It is a perfectly straightforward piece of work, albeit perhaps a little unusual in style. Besides, it is insulting to explain before the need arises and, as I learned with *Tiny Alice,* pointless after the need has, however arbitrarily, arisen.

All I think I need say about *Malcolm*—for those of you who do not know Purdy's work—is that the book is deeply sad and terribly funny, and I certainly hope that the play I have made from it will strike you as deeply sad and terribly funny, too. How I find it, at the moment, is of little value, for the play is all done, directed, costumed, set in place, well acted; and besides, my objectivity has gone the way of my sleep.

A few words on the matter of adaptation, itself, might not do any harm, though. (Might not do any good, either.) It was either John Simon or Robert Brustein—two critics-at-large of our culture whom I constantly get mixed up, so alike are they in their good-natured humility—who, in an observation that was most probably a paraphrase from somebody else, remarked that if adaptation from one medium to another was possible, then it wasn't worth doing.

I would agree that the majority of adaptations which arrive on our stages, be they adaptations of novels or European plays, are worthless, either through ineptitude or distortion, but it would be negligent to forget that much of the work of such pretty fair playwrights as Sophocles, Shakespeare, Racine, Giraudoux, and Anouilh has been adaptation.

No, the trouble with most of the stage adaptation we get in New York these years is that it is the work either of professionals who are hacks or learned men who are not theater professionals. Many third-rate novels have been made into third-rate plays of late, and a number of superior European plays have, in adaptation, been "Americanized" to the point where they have sunk mid-Atlantic.

Adaptation can be a perfectly respectable occupation for a playwright and, more important, a valid artistic act. And, naturally, no self-respecting playwright would, unless the roof were falling in on him and his, set about to adapt anything which (1) he did not respect as a work of art and (2) which he did not feel to be in line with his own aesthetic.

The responsibility of the playwright, when he becomes adapter, is double—to the work adapted, and to the stage as an art form. He must sometimes alter a work radically, so that no change will seem to have taken place when it is moved from the page to the stage. He must make the work belong between curtains as much as it ever did between covers.

One of the greater pleasures I received when I made the adaptation of Carson McCullers's *The Ballad of the Sad Café* was to be thanked for putting the dialogue from the book so faithfully on the stage when, in truth, the book is without dialogue. And, parenthetically, one of the smaller annoyances was to get two letters the same day, one telling me I had changed McCullers's novella too much, the other too little. But the pleasures of working on *The Ballad of the Sad Café* far outweighed the sorrows—for me, at any rate—and the fact that the piece was far more of a critical success than a commercial one is just so much of a shrug.

With James Purdy's book, I have wandered further, in specifics, than I did with McCullers's, but I have come back as far, and while I'm sure I'll get letters telling me I have changed *Malcolm* both too much and too little, I will be pleased if *Malcolm* seems to have moved from the book to the theater without the help or hindrance of my art—seems, in other words, to belong where it is.

And I will be pleased even more if James Purdy's public increases as the result of *Malcolm* becoming a play.

CREATIVITY AND COMMITMENT

1966

THE ALTERNATIVES AVAILABLE to a group posting subjects for discussion by a gathering of writers such as the forthcoming International PEN Congress are simply put: keep the subjects general enough for each writer to find a spot for his personal preoccupations; keep them specific enough to give a sense of order to the inevitable generalized oratory.

Alternative nightmares are available, of course, should the writers do the unthinkable and hew to either project set them and, to a man, deliver themselves exclusively of either generalities or particulars—hot air or nitpicking.

But writers—good ones, at any rate—are both philosopher and scientist, and it was wise of the PEN planning board to include a little bit of everything.

I doubt there will be much argument over the propriety of the overall theme of the conference—"The writer as Independent Spirit"—unless, of course, our friends from mainland China show up. Oh, one might quarrel some over the word "independent," did not the subthemes anchor it enough to permit as much argument over the aptness of the particulars as over the definition of the general topic.

During a trip to the Soviet Union and Poland and Czechoslovakia and Hungary a couple of years ago, I found that conversations with writers and painters and other "intellectuals"—a term, by the way, used without much embarrassment in Europe—would, quite automatically, and without direction, turn, at one point or another, to the matter of the position of the creative artist in his community—his independence, his responsibilities, the function of the artist, the nature of free expression. A young man in one of those countries, one of the many people I met outside of my planned itinerary, put the fundamental matter of our concern quite casually at the end of an informal evening: "Look," he said, "none of it will matter anymore, the freedoms, the purposes, once, in a worldwide sense, the general semantics breaks down, once communication on concepts is lost."

The item, naturally, should be the subject for discussion at any internal gathering of writers, and doubtless it will be the concern this June, but implicitly, alas, for it is an area, one of the far too many, controlled ultimately by the finger on the button and not on the typewriter key.

What can we say, in general, of the function of the writer, his position within and outside his society, his nature? Well, perhaps we had better examine the differences between good and bad writers. Good writers define reality; bad ones merely restate it. A good writer turns fact into truth; a bad writer will, more often than not, accomplish the opposite. A good writer writes what he believes to be true; a bad writer puts down what he believes his readers believe to be true. The good writer believes the intellectual and moral responsibility of his audience to be equal to his own; the bad writer considers the opposite posture proper. The popularity of a piece of writing will always tell you more about the state of critical letters and public taste than it will about the excellence of the work.

These conditions are stable, of course, have been for centuries, and no one expects them to be changed for the better. A holding action is possible, though, against public intellectual sloth, and less possible, though still conceivable, against governmental dictatorship, be it either consciously imposed as a national or international program of long-term and grandiose goal, or as a temporary expedient. But what of the various challenges to the writer as independent spirit suggested by the subthemes to be discussed at the PEN conference about to begin? *Does* the writer as politically committed animal do damage to "his true creative impulse"? God knows, a look to American writing of the thirties would lead us to think it damn well can, but at the same time, no writing, save carefully controlled escapism, can avoid such a commitment, however implicit or filtered it may be. Are creative writers making society rather than man himself their subject, leaning too heavily on the social sciences and psychology? Can we make use of facts—the ingredients of truth—without becoming their servants? *Will* Marshall McLuhan explain the new "theory of communication" and "the writer in the electronic age" so that I (at least) will finally be able to sense the subject through all the electrical discharge?

And, most interestingly of all, will the discussion of these subjects and the larger and smaller matters they relate to interest anyone other than writers? While it is true that the good writer creates his audience, and the bad writer creates himself out of the whole cloth of his view of himself as perpetuator of the intellectual status quo, creativity cannot breathe in a total vacuum. If the matters we are to discuss are of no interest to those about whom we write—for whom we take the trouble, if you will permit—then we'd better have another conference right quick, to find out whether or not our spirit has become independent of everything.

THE FUTURE BELONGS TO YOUTH

1967

WITH A NEW PLAY of mine opening its doors to the critics a couple of days from now, I daresay I should be so obsessed with it that an article about its merits and intentions would more or less type itself out. Such, though, is not the case. I don't mean to suggest that I'm bored with the play (it's called *Everything in the Garden,* by the way) or that I find it not worth talking about; indeed, it's not a boring play at all and its concerns are of considerable interest to me, and it may be that my involvement with it is so complete at this point that much of an attempt to discuss it would be a disengagement.

Let me try for a bit, though, and then move on to something else. Two young British playwrights died this year—Joe Orton and Giles Cooper. Orton was murdered and Cooper was killed in an accident. The death of a playwright is always a serious matter, for we always have too few good ones, and both these men were good. They did not die the way most playwrights do—through indifference or misunderstanding—but absurdly. I mourn them both.

They had important things in common. Most important (and the least common), they shared the view of life as a tragic comedy and were able to write hilariously about sad and bitter matters. Neither wrote perfectly (thank heavens!) for they sensed that our present dramatic structure is not always up to today's drama and they knew the playwright's responsibility to wrest change not only in an audience's apprehension of the world about it, but in the form of the art as well. They were both on their way to becoming important to us.

Giles Cooper's play, *Everything in the Garden,* came to my attention a couple of years ago when my coproducer, Clinton Wilder, suggested that we might want to produce it in New York. The play had been received oddly in London (outrage, delight, confusion) and while I found it neither outrageous nor confusing, I *was* delighted by it. We decided that a little carpentry should be done, nothing more, really, than resetting it in the United States and altering British expressions to American ones. Oh, a few other things but not much.

My work on the play was to be more or less invisible, and I saw no need for my name to appear on the program. Then something happened, and by the time I was finished with my work there was hardly a word left of the original. This was neither madness nor immodesty on my part, but merely that Cooper's play became a catalyst and set me to working my own variations on his theme. So, what will open this Wednesday is not an adaptation of another man's work but a much more intense collaboration. Giles Cooper and I never met, unfortunately, but I feel I know him very well.

Perhaps his play is better than mine; perhaps it is not. I can only say that our work has become enmeshed to the point that I can no longer tell where his leaves off and mine begins.

The actors (Barbara Bel Geddes, Barry Nelson, Beatrice Straight, and Robert Moore, to name just four) are super; Peter Glenville's direction strikes me as being just right; and I am terribly proud of Giles Cooper. Starting on Thursday the critics will begin to tell us whether or not we have a commercially successful play. And maybe a few of them will even tell us whether or not we have a good one.

Curiously enough, it is this confusion—this relating of commercial success to artistic which has made such a mire of the Broadway theater (and has corrupted off-Broadway, too, unfortunately)—which has prompted the beginnings of something interesting in the American theater. For the first time I sense the incipiency of a healthy revolution. A whole new generation of playwrights is turning its back on the commercial theater in order to work as it wishes, and a whole new generation of theatergoers has come up with the education to know good from bad. And I doubt any of this would have happened had the commercial theater not slipped a rung or two below mediocrity.

I spend a fair amount of time each year talking with students at colleges around the country, and—unless these kids fall asleep in the head as soon as they graduate—they really know what the theater is about. They know about Beckett, and Genet, and Brecht, and Pinter and they know that this theater is the truly contemporary one. They want a theater which engages rather than disengages; they want to be shook up, and not placated; they want the theater to be tough, and intense, and adventuresome; they want questions and not merely answers. They are offended by the majority fare on Broadway because they want to become more aware of themselves and not less.

They are going to be a tough audience, and I suspect the

commercial theater is going to have to accommodate itself to them sooner or later. These young people are not staying away from the main body of the theater these days because of the economics; they are staying away because most of our theater doesn't have anything to do with anything.

Most.

But not all. The second generation of new American playwrights (if we go back a few years and think of Gelber, and Kopit, and Richardson and some others as the first) is doing some of the most interesting writing we've had in the American theater in a long while. Also some of the worst, and quite often simultaneously. The Sam Shepards, and the Lanford Wilsons, and Adrienne Kennedys, and Paul Fosters, and all the others who are writing in such an explosion these days are concerned with nothing less than changing the face of the theater, redefining the nature of the theatrical experience. And they are not trying to do it on Broadway, of course. They are finding a congenial atmosphere for experiment in the coffeehouses, and they are finding a greater understanding and acceptance of their work in Europe than they are here.

It is rash to predict, of course, but I suspect that within the next five or ten years a new kind of theater is going to emerge in the United States, and that it will have an audience ready for it. The experiments are going on now, and they are often messy, and they often fail, and the search for new forms may give the appearance of an inability to deal with conventional ones, but it can never be any other way; such a radical shaking up is bound to leave things lying all over the floor.

Our theater is in for a violent change, and who knows, the day may even come when Harold Pinter won't have to play to half-empty houses on Broadway.

. . . APARTHEID IN THE THEATER

1967

WHEN I SAW Frank Marcus's play, *The Killing of Sister George*, a couple of years ago in London, my feelings about it were various: it was clear that Mr. Marcus was a playwright of far more than average interest—he had a certain savagery, a nice sense of the ironic, a firm enough command of past forms to play loose with them, a keen ear, a good feeling for parodistic sentimentality and a pleasing general irreverence.

At the same time, my delight with much of Mr. Marcus's play was lessened by a nagging feeling that *The Killing of Sister George* was trying to have the best of both worlds—to be brave and yet safe; to be outrageous and yet commercial; to give us a feeling that we have lived dangerously yet really wanting to leave us without a scar. (I don't mean to suggest—if my reactions to the play are anywhere near the truth of the matter—that there was any mendacity on Mr. Marcus's part, necessarily; it may be that in this particular piece he saw his art that way.)

I mention my reactions to *The Killing of Sister George* for they are similar to my reactions to Mr. Marcus's essay explaining his decision to permit performances of his work before segregated audiences in South Africa. Mr. Marcus says, at the tail of his article, "By and large, I think I acted correctly, but ultimately it's a matter for one's conscience."

And so it is with art. "By and large, I think I wrote correctly, but ultimately it's a matter of one's aesthetic." (Bad art is automatically immoral—to slip to one side for a moment—but accusations of immorality do not automatically make a work of art bad.)

No one—and certainly not Mr. Marcus—can be sanguine about the state of affairs in South Africa. The government is repressive, unrepresentative, authoritarian, and given grimly and undauntingly to the detestable policy of apartheid. And while it is possible that the whole problem of "what to do about South Africa" may be solved in a blood bath (13 million Africans against 3.5 million whites), it is more likely that democratic governments and individuals with the freedom to act will have to deal with the present totalitarian white-supremacist leadership for a long time to come.

Many, many playwrights—British, American, others, this writer among them—have protested the segregationist policies of the South African government by forbidding the performance of their plays before any but fully integrated audiences. Mr. Marcus suggests that this gesture is empty, that it succeeds merely in making the subscribers to it feel "self-denying and virtuous." Mr. Marcus goes on to say that dictatorships thrive on isolation and become even more tyrannical when cut off from the world. Mr. Marcus finds similarity between the present situation in South Africa and the conditions in Nazi Germany where, he quite persuasively if none too accurately points out, the clandestine sounds of freedom were a woe to the Hitler government and a comfort to the oppressed Germans.

There is much to some of what Mr. Marcus says—but not enough. In Nazi Germany, to use his example, the Hitler government went about its grotesque and loathsome business with the approval, tacit or otherwise, of the vast majority of the population, while in South Africa, a small minority subjugates an overwhelming proportion of the people. This white minority supports its government (exceptions, of course) with enthusiasm and—from what I have been able to judge in conversation with white segregationist South Africans—True Belief.

The white population of South Africa is not to be enlightened by the showing of plays by Harold Pinter, or Samuel Beckett, or Arthur Miller, or me—or Frank Marcus. It is the oppressed African population which needs, to quote Mr. Marcus again, "some spark, some message from across the border."

I, for one, have no objection to a white segregationist in South Africa seeing my plays, to be uplifted or thrown down by them (choose your critic) so long as an African from that same sad country is free to receive the same "spark."

I don't believe a writer can have a double standard. I do not permit the performance of my plays in the United States except before fully integrated audiences (a stand which blacks in this country will have to tell me is right, or not) and I see no reason to permit segregated performances of my plays in a foreign country, either.

If South Africans wish to put on the plays of writers who feel as I do, then South Africa will have to withdraw from the Copyright League.

* * *

Mr. Marcus is right in one of his points—when he suggests that a gesture by certain playwrights is not enough. (If this were not a theater article, I would advocate the boycott of South Africa by United States tourists and—laughable thought?—American business.)

I suggest the following action in the United States as a step toward correcting the present inadequacy of the gesture of a few:

1) U.S. playwrights, through the Dramatists Guild and otherwise, en masse, forbid the performance of their plays before segregated audiences anywhere within the Copyright League.

2) U.S. playwrights forbid the sale of their plays to the films unless there is a clause permitting the showing of these films in integrated theaters only.

3) The Screen Actors Guild, the Screen Writers Guild, and the Screen Directors Guild make a similar stand. (In this area, there will be a lot of pussyfooting, but the action can be taken if the screen actors, directors, and writers are adamant.)

4) American performers—singers, instrumentalists, orchestras, stand-up comedians, all—refuse to perform before segregated audiences.

If these loopholes were plugged, then I think we would be able to judge whether such a policy were to the benefit of the majority population of South Africa. I agree with Mr. Marcus that noble, partial gestures are meaningless in critical situations, but I suggest that a full-throated silence, so to speak, a world boycott by the arts (I have given up on the business community as I trust I made clear earlier) might reach the waxy ears of the white minority in South Africa.

It has been said that the second half of the twentieth century—if we get through it—will see the end of Caucasian supremacy in the world and the coming to dominance of "the black and yellow skins," as a southern U.S. senator had it once. If this is so—and the world certainly couldn't be run much worse than it gives the impression of being right now—or even if it is not, or if the theory is an oversimplification, I see no reason why the artist need make the same compromises that his government, in the name of realpolitik, feels *it* must during and contributing to this indicated decline of the West.

The toleration and even active support by the United States of governments such as those of Batista in Cuba, Chiang Kai-shek in China, Farouk and Co. in Egypt have had their predictable results, and our inaction (in the name of sweet reason) in the cases of Duvalier in Haiti, Smith in Rhodesia, and Vorster in South Africa, to mention just a few, will probably give us something further to answer for.

For a revolutionary society with some pretty good principles to export, our record is rather spotty, and I see no reason why individuals in the United States—playwrights and others—should not take the actions our government probably daydreams it was taking.

Playwrights of the world unite! You have nothing to lose except your South African royalties!

The Decade of Engagement

1970

TOWARD THE END of 1969 I had my most recent dream about the end of the world. It is a dream I have about once a year—a rather calm dream—and it cannot be fairly called a nightmare. For while the extinction of life on earth by fire and suffocation is nightmare material, the result of such a holocaust—the earth becoming like its moon—produces an intense sadness rather than terror.

Nightmares are made of what has happened or what we can conceive happening. Dreams do not have to be.

In this dream, I am on a beach by the ocean. It is dusk turning rapidly into night. I am with two or three friends, none of whom is anyone I can place on waking. We are lying about, and perhaps we have a driftwood fire smoldering. It is incredibly quiet—rather as if all sound had been turned off. And suddenly it begins: an area of the eastern horizon is lighted by the fired explosion, hundreds of miles away, and no sound at all. Then another, perhaps to the west, no sound. Within seconds they are everywhere, always at a great distance.

To the three or four of us on the beach, before our smoldering fire, there is no question as to what is happening: we are watching the end of the world. There is no time for terror; it is overleaped, and the suddenness is unimaginable as the silent bombs go off. It will be seconds before our own lives cease—or maybe we are already dead; perhaps that is why there is no sound.

So much for the dream. I dare say I shall continue to have it until either the world dies or I do.

Coming as it did, though, at the last few breaths of the decade, the dream reminded me that we have, in fact, survived the 1960s and, having done so, stand a chance—or so the balance-of-terror people will have us believe—of getting through the 1970s. Good luck to us all.

Amid the sighs of relief that accompany the end of a decade rises the chatter of typewriter keys. Almost anyone of a literary and/or journalistic turn takes the occasion to look fore and aft, to suggest what is likely to happen in the new decade, based on his view of the successes and wreckage of the one just concluded, and, if he is a grumbly sort, to complain a bit about the distance between the possible and the likely.

Of course, the questions can come up: Why should we even bother to concern ourselves with the state of the theater, for God's sake? Don't we have enough to worry about already? Are we not in a war that has divided this country more than any other since the Civil War? Are we not burdened with a government whose apparent concern with such matters as the Bill of Rights is dangerously minimal? In other words, given all that, and much else, is there any obligation on the part of anybody—save those who are either greedy or exhibitionistic or plain stupid enough to get involved with the theater in the first place—to concern himself with the state of the theater?

Well—greed and exhibitionism and plain stupidity aside—I think there is. The condition of the theater is always an accurate measure of the cultural health of a nation. A play always exists in the present tense (if it is a valuable one), and its music—its special noise—is always contemporary. The most valuable function of the theater as an art form is to tell us who we are, and the health of the theater is determined by how much of that we want to know.

I am less concerned than perhaps I should be with the specific ills and woes of the theater as a commodity market in the United States. I am far more concerned with what these symptoms suggest, for the only pertinence the theater has is as an art form, and the society in which it exists is—doubtless to the surprise of some—of more enduring importance than the economies of the commercial theater, the state of criticism, or who's going to play the lead next in *Hello, Dolly!*

For anyone who is interested in the grubbier side of the commercial theater in the United States, I recommend a volume by William Goldman entitled *The Season*. It is an informative book and brings to public attention much of the corruption—both economic and spiritual—of that commercial enterprise.

It is also, unfortunately, a book easily as corrupt as its subject—informative so long as one does not care any more than Mr. Goldman seems to about whether the information is true, half-true, or absolute fabrication—informative in the main, alas, if one's drive for knowledge is easily satisfied by such tactics as smear, snigger, and innuendo.

Mr. Goldman displays a compulsion to demean his betters, an unfailing attraction (intellectual or instinctual, I am not sure which) to the mediocre, and repeatedly makes embarrassingly hysterical references to that laughable nonsense—the takeover of the American Theater by homosexuals—references that, in their stridency, almost strike one as the attempts of a man to fortify himself against surprise attacks from within.

It is a shame that the book is not better—that its author's nature is such that what could have been a valuable piece of muckraking journalism emerges instead as opportunism. No one can fault Goldman for trying to make a buck, of course, and his book will probably make a swell musical; just think of the cast, with all those names Goldman drops things on.

I suspect that the 1960s will come to be thought of as the most exciting decade of American Theater to date—and one of the most depressing as well.

During the 1960s the serious theater found that it no longer had to attempt uncomfortable coexistence with the occasionally extremely skillful escapist entertainments that are the staple of the commercial theater on Broadway. Truly serious plays no longer had to compete with what generally passes for seriousness on Broadway—the *J.B.*s, *The Great White Hope*s, the *Rosencrantz and Guildenstern*s—but found that there were new arenas and new audiences.

Mind you, I'm not trying to suggest that serious plays cannot exist on Broadway, and will not continue to do so; with rare exceptions, their life expectancy is far less than that of the escapist entertainments or their middle-brow cousins. It is simply that during the 1960s an alternative became available. That alternative was, of course, off-Broadway, and the explosion of reality and public awareness of what the theater was really all about occasioned by its advent is undoubtedly the most important theatrical event of the 1960s.

People are always complaining that there aren't enough good playwrights. Well, of course, there never can be enough good playwrights, but concurrent with the first performances in the United States of the work of the European avant-garde—men such as Genet, Ionesco, and a giant named Beckett—there began emerging a generation of first-rate and potentially first-rate American playwrights, of a number and diversity I am not aware of having existed before in such a short period of time. To list just a few names: Jack Gelber, Arthur Kopit, Frank Gilroy, Jack Richardson, Sam Shepard, Lanford Wilson, Israel Horovitz, Leonard Melfi, Adrienne Kennedy, Paul Foster. Some of these will prove to be shooting stars, to be sure, but the fact of them is a wonder, nonetheless.

The 1960s also saw an eruption of repertory theaters throughout the country, aided by private foundations, as well as by the government, aware that perhaps the American Theater was beginning to come of age.

And in our universities we suddenly began to find that in theater courses the history of the theater no longer ended with Ibsen, and that university productions of serious avant-garde plays were becoming commonplace.

It was an exciting decade except that toward the end of it things began to turn a little sour. A retrenchment began—perhaps nothing more than the usual two-steps-forward-one-step-back syndrome—or perhaps a swinging away from adventure in our society, a confusion and dismay with the ways of the world. Our politics has swung toward reaction, our vocal youth are viewed with hostility, and the vast majority of the hundred million guns which are privately owned in this country are not in the hands of the militant blacks.

And the theater has suffered as a result. It may be—as it certainly seems to be in the minds of many—that reality is of such stuff that our arts must begin to serve us as we would have them do, to become mirrors of what we wish to see rather than of what is.

Art is not escape; it is engagement, and a general disengagement seems to me to be the greatest danger to the vitality of the arts in the 1970s.

A dialogue was begun in the 1960s—an essential dialogue—in which the public came to realize more than ever before that it was not enough to be either a passive recipient of the arts or a determinator of their nature, but that the arts were to be participated in with much the same engagement and sense of responsibility as that which motivated those who were creating them.

This dialogue must be renewed, for without it the arts will wither, and that is always the sign of a society that has turned in upon itself and is in the process of ceasing to matter.

MILTON AVERY

1978

AN EMINENT ART critic and historian wrote to me the other week, saying, "Avery is one of those artists who seem to me to say what they have to say so clearly that to write about their pictures must be either presumptuous or redundant."

Well, this gentleman happens to be not only an eminent critic, but a very good one, as well, as I suspect you will agree after you read his essay on Milton Avery which follows this brief preface of mine. In it, John Canaday puts his own misgivings to rest. Clearly, there is always something to say if you know how to say it. Mr. Canaday concentrates on those very elements of Avery's work which make him tricky to define and, at the same time, most identifiable.

It is possible, at a quick glance, to confuse a 1913 Braque with a Picasso of the same year; the constructivists can bewilder us a little as to just who is doing what; and I always have trouble keeping my fauves straight—there's one Matisse I just *know* is a Derain, for example.

But when Mr. Canaday writes of Avery that "each picture seems to have been created according to its own set of rules" and that "the artist remains a loner separated from both his sources and his descendants," he hits a nerve center that transmits Avery's qualities from mere excellence to something loftier.

I can't recall how I became aware of Avery's world. Was it a reproduction in an art magazine? Was it seeing that superb Paris painting at the Whitney? Was it during a visit to a small gallery on Waverly Place in Greenwich Village, in a conversation with its gentle and informed owner, Morris Weisenthal, when he showed me an Avery etching of a reclining female nude—elongated, distorted, simplified, brought down (up?) to its essence?

Perhaps it was none of these times, but soon enough after that found me—through the courtesy of the gentle Mr. Weisenthal—at Avery's apartment in New York City, meeting Milton and Sally Avery and being allowed to spend a quiet hour rummaging privately through a hundred or so canvases.

A quiet hour? Well, quiet in my awe, perhaps, but I was engulfed by color, a color sense that I personally find relating most closely to the Japanese woodcut, a bravery and surprise of color that Munch also occasionally achieved.

I was hooked. I was young and quite poor at the time, and while Avery's prices in those days were still a laugh, I could afford only one painting. I chose a canvas of two sprawled figures—one ghostly white, the other Avery blue, on a brown field—and went industriously back to my desk to write another play so that I could get some more.

My tastes in art are catholic, and I have gone on in many directions as a collector, but in *my* rooms an Avery above a table on which might be a Jalisco piece, with a Kandinsky to the left and a Vuillard to the right, gives me a sense that all is in order.

Mark Rothko used to visit me from time to time, and we would talk of many things or merely listen to music. Mark would always place himself so that he was seated facing a wall of Averys. That was fine with me knowing how much Mark admired Avery's work. It was also fine because there was yet another Avery on a wall behind Rothko's chair, so I would have the two of them to look at while we talked.

LOUISE NEVELSON

1980

LOUISE NEVELSON HAS accomplished the age of eighty unflagged, undiminished as an artist, but with something curiously awry—the fame of her persona overshadows that of her work in the general public's mind.

I doubt there are any living American artists photographs of whom elicit more immediate public recognition than Nevelson's. Not even Warhol's retreating, appalled, oddly ghostlike image is more familiar to the casual reader of elegant or lowbrow junk than "the Nevelson"—the foot-long sable eyelashes framing the deep no-nonsense eyes, the coats of many colors, the splendid unexpected jewelry, the profound juxtapositions.

At the same time, I doubt if a majority of the celebrity conscious who can spot Nevelson in a group party photograph could relate the woman to the work. They may know what Nevelson looks like, but they don't know who she is.

The factors which make celebrities of some living creative artists and which keep others—their equals or betters, often as not—in relative shadow are complex. Certainly Hemingway sought the bright lights, the photo essays, the gossip-column mention as a natural (and naturally self-serving) extension of his sense of himself, as naturally as his coevals, Faulkner and Steinbeck, shy men of a private demeanor, found it unnatural. And while history has not yet proved (nor may it, ever) Hemingway a superior writer to the other two, goodness! he is a more famous one.

Examples abound in all the arts. The poet Allen Ginsberg, through his Beat association and his function as a performing poet, is more a public possession than either [the late] Muriel Rukeyser or John Ashbery—though Ashbery seems to be working at putting this to rights.

The composer Ned Rorem, through photographs, volumes of self-exposure, and through his penchant for publishing opinions on almost every subject, is more deeply embedded in the broad public consciousness than either Elliott Carter or George Crumb, two men whose music is doubtless at least the equal of Rorem's.

Warhol—the majority of whose work sells, I suspect, in direct relation to his maintained personal celebrity—is, to my mind's eye, a lesser artist than Jasper Johns or Clyfford Still, say, two whose dedication to the exploitation of their personas is touching in its absence.

But the public possession of the persona of the artist is not necessarily a denigrating sign. Picasso was, for most of his career, a better than first-rate painter, and "that face!" was probably better known than *Les Demoiselles d'Avignon* or *Night Fishing at Antibes.* The ghost of Juan Gris could, however, probably wander into a retrospective of his own work in a public gallery and be asked (politely, to be sure) if he was just browsing or wanted assistance.

Charisma—which is often nothing more than the conscious (or instinctive) desire to exploit the self—commodity as agent—probably misinforms a number of people about absolute values, but is a phenomenon which will be with us as long as the public prints realize it is what the people want (as opposed to what they should want), and in a consumer-oriented society, especially in a democracy, it can (and should) be no other way.

But what a bizarre picture of the arts—the creative mind—it tolerates, even encourages! I have watched the celebrity of creative artists blossom as their creativity withered, and others go on to do their best work long after the popular consumer thought they had died.

As often as not the public celebration of the creative artist is a combination of cynical media-exploitation and touchingly naive public homage—albeit to the symbol of the thing (the person) rather than to the thing itself (the work).

And this brings me back to Louise Nevelson, a bird of rare plumage, whose work, at its very best, is as good as any being done in the second half of this century, and whose art and persona are perhaps more the same thing—in the very best of senses—than any other living artist.

Were my response to Nevelson's work not sympathetic—did I not admire greatly a lot of her accomplishment—I would not be writing this introduction, would not have wanted to. At the same time, my reaction to Nevelson's art is doubtless idiosyncratic, and one or two of the conclusions I have come to may startle or dismay either the artist or her champions. Be that as it may, just as Nevelson was one of the few people who saw instinctively to the core of my play *Tiny Alice*, I can bring to bear on my appreciation of her art the whims of my own creative reasoning.

People who practice the arts bring to a discussion of the arts special information unavailable (except as hearsay) to the historian or aesthetician, information—or insight if you will—not necessarily as easily useful to the art-experience recipient as other views may seem but nonetheless often more congruent to the intended relationship of the art to the recipient. And since most art recipients are more interested in how art can be useful to their view of themselves rather than in the (I suspect) ultimately more valuable adversary experience through which art is instructive and is an act of aggression against the familiar and the "easy," very few creative artists are hired as critics in the popular and influential media.

But enough of this; on to the matter at hand.

A brief recapitulation of the Louise Nevelson story is in order.

In one way this is easy enough to put down on paper, for the outlines of the biography are already available to anyone who wants to read them—dates, events, exhibits, and so on—and there is a chronology elsewhere . . . which lists such compass markings.

There is a difficulty, though, for facts tell us little, and it is the meaning of facts—what produced them, what they produced—that makes most biography a little less accurate than most autobiography.

Nevelson has said, "I seek truth. What I seek is anything that will work for me; I'll use a lie if it works, and that [becomes] the truth." While Nevelson does not share Blanche DuBois's credo, "I tell you what ought to be true" (indeed, I know no person more candid than Nevelson about the implications of facts), she does share the commonly held view among creative artists that facts are less interesting than truth and that, given your lights, you can let a fact lead you into either a pit of darkness or almost blinding illumination.

Example: Nevelson writes that often she was on the verge of suicide (during the 1940s, for example). What truth is to be gained from this information?—that Nevelson was psychologically disturbed? or the far more useful and valuable information that Nevelson was frequently in despair during this period because she had not yet been able to release from within herself the art (or view of reality, whichever you like) she knew she contained, was possessed by.

What we make of facts is what we need from them, and the creative mind—which probably has access to the unconscious in ways the noninterpretive does not—understands the purpose of facts in ways we would be unwise not to learn from.

I suppose I could (were I that sort of person) betray the confidence Nevelson has placed in me as a friend, and speckle this essay with a hundred privileged anecdotes—what she "really" thinks of her contemporaries, what we talk about at a dinner party, what it's "like" to be with her—under the guise of revealing the person (therefore the artist). I *could* do it, and could, through careful selection, reveal Nevelson as saint or devil, but I would not. Friends, doctors, and priests have much the same code, and could I break bread with Nevelson again once having broken her trust?

Besides, except for the very young, creative people don't sit around and discuss aesthetics very much. They discuss themselves— by which I mean they discuss the matters of the world, mundane and otherwise, as seen through the doors of their own perception. This is very interesting to those who share those perceptions, and inexplicable to those who do not.

I have supped with Auden, looked at an ocean with Rothko, drunk wine with Beckett, watched Tennessee Williams swim forty lengths of my pool, gathered wood with Nevelson on the streets of Little Italy. On none of these occasions can I recall a *mot* or a profundity uttered. We were people at ease with one another: there were no reporters about; yet I could as easily say that I watched *In Praise of Limestone* knife through a steak, for example, was splashed as *Suddenly Last Summer* belly flopped (no pun intended), or watched an older woman stoop into a Prince Street gutter and come up with a work of art already—not yet, but already—black and inevitable.

The creator and the art are inseparable, once you have known them both.

I hope that I have revealed nothing too heady for the fan or too perplexing to the scholar already wrapped in his theories by having let it slip that Tennessee swims. For the clearest view of Nevelson I point you to her work. She is there.

It is interesting to briefly trace Nevelson's evolution from . . . [the anthropomorphic pieces of the 1930s] through "The Clown Is the Center of His World" show, 1943, to the work of the Nierendorf Gallery exhibit of 1944, to two major breakthroughs of the 1950s, and *First Personage* of 1956, to the first of the extensive environments, *Moon Garden + One* of 1958.

Unquestionably, there is an extraordinary maturing here, an eventual coming together, through all the influences—ancient and modern, folk and sophisticated, conscious and unconscious—to an ultimate star-burst statement. And it is gratifying that when the breakthrough came, when the art and artist fused, achieved harmony, there were gifted observers ready and eager to applaud. Dorothy Miller, Dore Ashton, Emily Genauer were there to proselytize and push, and, after the death of Nevelson's first real champion, the dealer Karl Nierendorf, another series of women,

Lotte Jacobi, Colette Roberts, and Martha Jackson, showed her work at their galleries.

Nevelson has suggested that she is the most feminine of artists: "I feel that my works are definitely feminine. There is something about the feminine mentality that can rise to heaven. The feminine mind is positive and not the same as a man's. I think there is something feminine about the way I work. A man simply couldn't use the means of, say, fingerwork to produce my small pieces. They are like needlework. . . ."

And while her reputation rests primarily on the large sculptural pieces and environments, Nevelson herself leans toward her graphics—especially the ones employing lace—as her most personal and even favorite creations.

But the idea of the sex of art troubles me. Certainly the terms cannot apply to the work of Henry Moore and Barbara Hepworth of the 1930s when they were both making brave explorations; and, indeed, Moore's work of the last twenty years can be read as less "masculine" than the gestures Hepworth was making right up to her killing accident. And Anne Ryan was a lesser collagist than Kurt Schwitters, not through any feminine muting of her color sense or any sexually determined structural muddiness, but simply because she was less innovative and had a less compelling creative intelligence.

It is interesting, though, that women have been such a strong force in U.S. art over the past forty years. A couple of valuable books have been appearing lately concerning themselves with first-rate U.S. artists who happen to be women, and I imagine that soon a revealing text about historically important women art dealers of the same period (Betty Parsons, Eleanor Ward, Rose Fried, Edith Halpern, Bertha Schaffer, Martha Jackson, for example) will emerge.

In any event, women of taste and authority were there when Nevelson was ready for them, and if their response to her work was affected by Nevelson's sex, it was, I am certain, unconscious, and it would be the first and only time such a consideration appears in their various judgments as critics and dealers. In fact, I am inclined to dismiss the suggestion as nonsense.

An understanding of Nevelson's oeuvre is possible only when one comprehends that what it has been attempting all along is something other than works of art, as the term is commonly understood. Oh, she has been creating works of art all along, individual and collective assemblages, but from the middle 1950s all of Nevelson's work, all her pieces, have been one enormous sculptural idea—or world, if you will.

This is not to suggest that the "parts" are any less interesting than the "sum." Indeed, on many occasions the reasoning is easily as interesting as the conclusion—to me, at any rate—for it can be a kind of miniature course in twentieth-century art history, a view of the sources which lead to the highly original result.

A word here is in order to clear up the quote in Arnold Glimcher's book [*Louise Nevelson*]—"Nevelson does not admit to conscious influences."

The truth, of course, is that Nevelson is neither a self-conscious primitive nor a fool; she knows that she, along with almost every other valuable artist, has been influenced by everything that she has seen, heard, touched. It is merely that her mind absorbs stimuli for later use without making a conscious checklist of the materials filed away. All matter we absorb is either nutriment or waste, and we treat it accordingly.

Did Nevelson's interest in African, Aztec, and Mayan art, folk weaving—fabrics of all kinds, in fact—affect her work? Of course;

sometimes directly (certainly neither more nor less than Picasso's first exposure to African sculpture "blew his mind," as they say these days) and sometimes only to the extent of broadening—ordering—her perceptions.

And what do we say of the family resemblances between individual statements by Nevelson and certain pieces by Schwitters, Picasso, Vantongerloo, and even Torres-Garcia? Did Nevelson know these works? Was she consciously influenced by them? Does it matter? If we are not influenced (directly or indirectly) by a specific important art statement, the chances are very great that we *have* been influenced either by its precedents or successors.

The very best of Nevelson's individual assemblages, or structures, or sculptures (or drawings, as she has referred to them) are, variously, exquisite, powerful, remote, primordial, and always intellectually stimulating. They do things to the mind akin to what a Bach two- or three-part invention does.

But it is when these singularities are combined, joined in company to many others—assemblage of assemblage—that they accumulate an emotional intensity that is the essence of Nevelson's specialness.

Let me take *Mrs. N's Palace* as a case in point. Of all the structures . . . [created in recent decades], it is the only one which can swallow us up in the actual experience of it. With the others—*Dawn's Wedding Feast* or *The Royal Voyage,* for example—one can be surrounded, one can move through or past, but the *Palace* is the only one in which one literally enters Nevelson's world, is engulfed by it.

My first experience of this piece (or work) was emotionally as well as intellectually involving—intensely so on both levels. I had a similar experience a few years earlier; I sat in the reconstruction of a room Mondrian had designed; imagine a Mondrian painting twenty by twenty feet; then imagine it a cube; then imagine yourself placed in the center of the cube. On both occasions, I had been transformed from spectator to participant. (I suspect Schwitters' *Merzbau* and Kiesler's *The Endless House* would have been related experiences.)

Nevelson tells me that she is a trifle bothered by *Mrs. N's Palace* because it is the only one of the large environments which is made up of pieces made at many different periods of time (1964–1977). All of the others (*The Royal Voyage*, 1956, for example) are, at least in theory, of a stylistic unity, but it is this very catalogue of Nevelsonia that is *Mrs. N's Palace* that makes it for me not only an enriching and stimulating experience but a touching one as well. When I enter that piece, when I walk around it, when I examine the (how many!?) individual elements, I have the sense of being in the presence of the complete Nevelson. To mangle the Bach simile (but I don't care)—in the presence of so many of the inventions I am also in the presence of one of the great fugues.

Nevelson feels that she began making her "worlds" as an alternative space, so to speak—to create for herself a fathomable reality in the midst of the outside chaos. What has happened, of course, is that the private has become public, the refuge accessible to all, and, to those who know what a Nevelson looks like, the world is beginning to resemble her art.

I hope she's pleased.

Conversation with *Catch*

Catch: I guess the best way to start is for you to give us a brief background of your work in the arts and, in particular, your work in the theater so that our readers will have some kind of forum.

Albee: All right. I'm a playwright. I've been one since 1959. I have written nineteen plays. I suppose I could list them in some sort of order, if I wanted to. Like: *The Zoo Story, The Death of Bessie Smith, American Dream, The Sandbox, Who's Afraid of Virginia Woolf?, The Ballad of the Sad Café, Tiny Alice, Malcolm, A Delicate Balance, Everything in the Garden, All Over, Seascape, Counting the Ways* and *Listening, The Lady from Dubuque* and *Lolita*—in that vague order. I think I've left a couple of plays out—I always do—which brings us up to the present. I also direct—my own work and other people's. I write essays on theater and on art criticism—essays *of* art criticisms, actually. I curate exhibits of contemporary painting and sculpture. I run a foundation which gives residence to deserving young painters, sculptors, and writers. And that's about all anyone might need to know about me.

Catch: In your discussion last night, you insisted that the arts were as healthy as they had ever been and that it was the patronage of them that was declining. Is this a worldwide phenomenon, or do you see it as mainly an American one? And, secondly, is it symptomatic of only social or political conditions, or is there something in the art being produced that limits its appeal to the general public?

Albee: I'll reiterate what I said—that I do believe that there is as much worthwhile, interesting, and innovative art being produced in the United States now as there was twenty years ago, when the audience participation was far healthier. A lot's happened in twenty years: we've lost a great deal of self-confidence as a country and as a society. People are turning inward; they wish to vanish into their society. Notice what's happening on campuses right now. More and more students want to get the degree and disappear into the society and find a cushy job. Individuality seems to be not as highly regarded as it was. And when you have that particular kind of condition—the desire to conform, the desire to be a part of the society rather than healthily outside the society—you get a situation in which the arts are in trouble, because it is the function of art to protest the *status quo*—to try to change people, to try to bring them into a greater sense of themselves, make them more alive, more self-aware. And when people don't want that information they participate less in the art experience—which in no way means that artists are not participating in their society as they always did. The society is not participating in the arts to the extent that it did.

There's always the danger, I suppose, that if the arts realize that nobody's paying attention, that they will become hermetic, that they will be written or composed or painted or sculpted only for the people who are paying attention. But as I look around I don't see—especially in the theater—that they are. There are enough playwrights who are enormously socially involved, who are writing works of commentary, protest, and elucidation for an audience that, alas, is not paying the attention that it might. So I don't think that the arts have suffered yet from the lack of public participation, though ultimately they may.

Catch: My next question deals with nonrepresentational art in the theater—the avant-garde theater in America—and its upsurge in the sixties. A lot of the experimental, avant-garde work done in the sixties was an attempt to provide a more visceral, less intellectualized approach to art. The Living Theater, for example, strove for a more mythic, precultural approach to its subject matter. And yet this was not considered valid in terms of real-life experience by a lot of people who could most benefit from that art. I guess I'm looking for a grassroots theater in America, and I'm not seeing one. Do you think that, by working in the avant-garde, we are cutting off those people who could most benefit from the artistic experience?

Albee: Let's go back. There has always been an avant-garde—and first of all we have to define what the avant-garde is. The avant-garde is misnamed. It is not necessarily something that is in the forefront. The avant-garde is basically something which stands to one side of the conventional—that comments on it. It is very seldom in front. Uh, it becomes in front after it has made its comment and then people veer in its direction. It is not a straight line, in other words. There has always been an avant-garde. Shakespeare was an avant-garde playwright. So was Molière. So was Ibsen. So was Chekhov. So was Beckett. Any playwright who—or any artist in any field—who *changes* the nature of the art is avant-garde. Now you're referring, specifically, in your question to certain theater movements in the sixties and continuing through the seventies in the United States: the Living Theater, Grotowski's Theater in Poland, the Theater of—um, oh dear, I can never remember his name, that very good—Chaikin, Joe Chaikin . . . Joe Chaikin's Experimental Theater, and a number of experimental theaters that have functioned, not only in the United States, but in Europe in the past fifteen or twenty years, the basic emphasis of which has been to move the theater in the direction of the unconscious rather than the conscious, to move it away from intellectualized discussion, to move it into the really primordial areas of the unconscious. It's succeeded rather well. Grotowski manages to create a theater without a word, without a coherent word being spoken. When Joe Chaikin and Jean-Claude van Itallie worked together in the early seventies and did a piece on Genesis, the first book of The Bible, they created a language which was incomprehensible except to the unconscious. When Peter Brook made his large experiment in the Shah's Iran on a mountaintop with a forty-eight-hour play, he and his actors invented a language that nobody had ever spoken before in an attempt to get at the unconscious.

This has been the basic direction of what's happened in the experimental theater. And all experiments in the experimental and avant-garde theater are interesting, but almost all of them are partial theater. They must come back, ultimately, to a more coherent form of communication once they have made their experiments and freed the audience from its limitations on relying only upon conscious stimuli, then the theater can revert to its full usage, which includes words, which includes intellectualization, and all the rest. Most of the experiments are enormously interesting, but they're experiments in partial theater. You're looking for a grassroots theater? Well, you will have a grassroots theater when the grass roots are interested in having a theater. We are not a theater culture in this country. With the exception of a couple of playwrights—Clifford Odets and maybe Lillian Hellman—we didn't have a real live theater in this country until after the Second World War, when Tennessee Williams and Arthur Miller sprang up—and we had O'Neill, of course, in the thirties—but for the public consciousness theater didn't really exist until after the Second World War. And by that time, theater and movies and television— movies certainly—were the popular entertainment, and by the middle fifties, television was the popular entertainment. Theater has always been a minority participation. It is my feeling that television, and to a certain extent movies, are so terrible that they will drive people out into the streets . . . and possibly into the theater, which would be nice.

If people want live theater they will have it, but as long as people want theater to be escape rather than engagement, tell lies rather than truths, you're not going to have a grassroots theater. Theater is a minority participation because it tends—like the string quartet is a minority participation (um, rock music is very popular, string quartets are very unpopular). I would submit—from all the value that rock music may have, that, though it's been touted as a kind of folk culture where I think it is not . . . I think it is folk ripoff basically, basically the best example of folk ripoff being Mr. Dylan, for example . . . millions and millions and there's not a word of comprehensible sense in the past ten years. Oh dear, I get involved in these long sentences and then I forget what my point is. Um, yes. The string quartet, I would submit, is probably more instructive than the performance of a rock band. It probably teaches us a little bit more about order, about thinking, about using the mind in a linear, interesting fashion in a way that it has not been used before. It probably is a better experience, ultimately, and a more interesting experience. It is participated in by very, very few people; there is a prejudice against it. I'm convinced that we can have folk culture equated to the most serious culture any time we get rid of our prejudices. The same people who go to hear a piece of contemporary music in a concert hall by . . . who—Anton Webern, say, or any of the more contemporary composers—and are terribly upset by the sounds, and think it's awful sound. Those same people go to the movies, and they hear exactly those same chords in scores, and it doesn't bother them a bit. The same people who go to a gallery or a museum and see a painting by Jackson Pollock and think it's junk and nonsense—they see the same kind of work used in commercial advertising, and it doesn't bother them at all. So the whole thing is context, is it not, rather than the thing itself. So I'm convinced that the only thing that is holding serious art from being our folk culture is a curious kind of prejudice on the part of the participants.

Catch: Yes. One of the more interesting cases that just dropped into my mind is people who go to see, for instance, Kubrick's *2001,* go out and buy the soundtrack album and skip over all the tracks by Ligeti.

Albee: Mmm-hmm. True.

Catch: Thinking of Kubrick makes me think of *Lolita,* your play. It's been commented, by Gerald Mast, I believe, that Kubrick's movie was a failure because of the nature of the book it was adapted from, because that book depended on its first-person narrator and the vagaries of his use of language so heavily. Did you, in preparing for *Lolita,* come up against the same problem?

Albee: I don't know. I don't know whether I've solved the problem yet. I will be told. But judging by the audience response in New York I would seem to have solved it by avoiding a great deal of first-person narrative. When you dramatize something you have to dramatize that which is narrative. The failures of the Kubrick film of *Lolita* struck me as being, primarily, a misunderstanding of what the book was all about. And also miscasting. James Mason, who's a very good actor, has always been fifty-seven, and Humbert Humbert is meant to be thirty-eight. And the girl, Sue Lyon, who was playing Lolita, was capable of playing sixteen, but was incapable of playing twelve. The film was made at a time when there was a certain amount of self-censorship in Hollywood and various specific sections and specifics could not be discussed and so the movie ended up not being about many of the things that the book was about. I thought the movie was quite terrible. I thought Peter Sellers was allowed to run rampant and perform in a style that had nothing to do with the rest of the acting in the film. Nabokov himself had written a screenplay, and you will notice on the film that he is given screenplay credit, though they did not use his screenplay. I suspect had they used his screenplay they might have had a somewhat better film. There are lots of people who have tried to dramatize *Lolita.* The film failed, I think. There was a musical comedy version of it done by no less a person than um—Oh, who wrote *My Fair Lady*?

Catch: Lerner and Loewe?

Albee: Um. Yes. Alan Jay Lerner tried to do a musical version of *Lolita* that closed out of town. Perhaps my dramatization of *Lolita* will be only the most recent calamity, who's to say? I'm not sure. Though I think I may have caught some of the essence of it. It's always tricky to dramatize a book. When I did the adaptation of Carson McCullers's *Ballad of the Sad Café,* the critic for the *New York Daily News,* in his morning review after the opening, said that Albee didn't really have to do very much when he did this adaptation, all he did was put down on stage all of the dialogue from the book. And that interested me greatly because there is no dialogue in the book. And so I don't know whether I've succeeded or not. I like to think I have. I've tried to be faithful to Nabokov and faithful to myself.

Catch: Well, regardless, you seem to have received a lot of negative press about the play. Do you have anything to say to those people trying to strangle the play in the crib?

Albee: Well, we've received press in Boston. We received about twelve reviews and I think it was nine favorable and three unfavorable, but the unfavorable ones naturally got the most play. It was suggested that the play was salacious, obscene, perhaps. Well, that's Boston for you.

Catch: Aside from the press, you've been having problems with a Women's League Against Pornography, for example.

Albee: Oh, apparently they did something yesterday in New York.

Catch: What was that?

Albee: Well, I don't know. I'm told they were going to picket us in New York. They were going to complain that the play was about incest. Obviously, they've never seen the play or read the book, because the play does not concern itself with incest, nor is it pornographic. They're just trying to get some mileage for themselves. The play is a highly moral work. The book is a highly moral work. There is nothing pornographic or salacious about either the play or the book. So much for paying attention to what you read. Experience the thing itself.

Catch: The thing that I find most interesting about *Lolita,* in terms of your work as a whole, is that it represents the first time in a great while that you've dealt directly with sexuality in your work.

Albee: Really?

Catch: In *The Zoo Story,* in *The Death of Bessie Smith,* in *The Ballad of the Sad Café,* right up through *Tiny Alice,* the sexual drives of the characters seem to be one of the primary forces working in their lives. In later plays, *A Delicate Balance,* to a certain extent *The Lady from Dubuque, All Over* certainly, sexuality has left these people. They're menopausal almost, and almost afraid of sex in some cases. I think of *Listening* as an example.

Albee: Well, in *Listening* we have a girl who is a highly sexual animal, and part of her problem, her psychiatric problem, is repressed sexuality. Uh, I think in *Seascape,* two of the characters, Leslie and Sarah, the lizards, have a very healthy and active sex life. And indeed, the female of the two human characters is protesting the departure of their sex life.

Catch: Perhaps what I'm referring to is the use of sexuality as really a driving force in a person's life.

Albee: Well, when you write about people of a certain age—as I did in *All Over*—we are in a postsexual situation. If I write about younger people or different people then I write sexually, because their drive is sexual. It depends upon the circumstances. It's the same thing with style. Some plays give the illusion of being fairly naturalistic, others are highly stylized. It depends upon the stylistic exigencies of the work, as it is with the psychological and the sociosexual exigencies. It depends upon the circumstance.

Catch: Have you found yourself, in your more recent plays, uh, wanting to deal with an older person, a more mature person?

Albee: No, no. In *Seascape,* I imagine Leslie and Sarah are probably thirty and twenty-five—that's reasonably young. The girl in *Listening* is, I would imagine, about twenty-two, twenty-three—she's reasonably young. In *The Lady from Dubuque,* six of the eight characters are in their twenties and thirties—they're pretty young. You may have a point, but it's not supported by facts.

Catch: Is there a compelling reason to, say, adapt another person's work rather than, at the particular moment, put down something that's going on in your head?

Albee: No. No compelling reason, unless perhaps it seems interesting to do, it seems like an interesting challenge, and one
should meet that challenge. I mean, there was this enormous
mountain called *Lolita,* and I thought I should try to scale it.
You know, if something is an interesting challenge, well do it.

Catch: Seems a simple enough reason.

Albee: Well, you have to add to that the fact that it seems scalable,
and seems worth doing.

Catch: You've directed your own work. Have you ever had the
desire to act in it?

Albee: I stopped acting when I was about nineteen, twenty, when
I got thrown out of college. I did act for about ten years. I
don't know. I suspect I'm still a reasonably good actor, but I
don't really know that I want to get on the stage again . . .
and having to say all those boring words by *me* over and
over again . . . I don't know if I want to do that. Also, I like
a certain amount of freedom of movement, and if you're
acting, you're stuck in one place for a long time. Having said
that, I will probably be onstage next fall.

Catch: And we'll hold this up to you. . . . Inasmuch as the
Broadway theater seems shackled by commercial demands,
have you ever considered abandoning that forum and
thought of writing your plays for a fresh audience—perhaps
doing regional theater?

Albee: Sure. Everybody thinks about that. But the problem is this:
Why become a second-class citizen? Why burden yourself
economically into second-class citizenship? If everybody
who wrote serious plays gave up Broadway theater and
worked in something as congenial as university theater or
regional theater, the misinformation about the nature of

theater the Broadway theater gives to the rest of the United States would be complete. There have to be *some* people who still try to say, "Look here, theater is more complex than musicals and escapist comedies." Somebody has got to stay in there and do some fighting.

Catch: And yet it's not the most fruitful arena, say, for a fresh playwright.

Albee: No. Not necessarily. And yet somebody's got to do it. I mean Pinter does it, Shaffer does it, I do it, Williams does it, Miller does it. We keep trying, because, I think, we have a sense of responsibility to people's understanding of what theater's about. There could, conceivably, come a time (I don't think there will) when the standards that now apply to regional theater will be the Broadway standards. I'm convinced, for example, that if a miracle could occur and for the next ten years there was enough money supplied by somebody so that only the very best plays filled all the Broadway theaters, and none of the junk was allowed to be on Broadway, at the end of that ten-year period excellence would be the standard of the Broadway audience. I'm sure the standard would change. It's the combination of greed and cowardice on the part of the people who are mounting these plays on Broadway that gives us so many terrible ones.

Catch: Wouldn't you then have more artistic freedom, perhaps, if you didn't have to mount a million-dollar production, if you could experiment with a fifty-thousand-dollar production?

Albee: I don't think so, necessarily. A playwright can hold to his standards whether the producer's spending a million or fifty thousand. It's more *difficult* for a serious play to be put on Broadway all the time as the costs mount. And it's quite probable that within the same ten-year period that I've been talking about where the miracle could occur (which will not occur), it's more likely that at the end of this ten-year period there will be no serious plays on Broadway and all serious playwrights will have become second-class citizens. It's a pity. One shouldn't be penalized for using one's head.

Catch: How long do you see this trend of relatively light and long-running shows such as *Annie* and *A Chorus Line* and *Sugar Babies* going on while you're reportedly having such a difficult time scaring up financial backing for *Lolita*?

Albee: Well, I didn't. The producer did . . . because he's a lunatic, a dangerous amateur who brings a combination of arrogance and ignorance to his job as a producer, uh, but now I should say something terrible about him probably, having said all the nice things. I imagine *that* would be complete, as I say, in ten years. You won't *have* a serious play on Broadway in ten years. *Chorus Line* will still be running, Neil Simon will still be churning out his escapist entertainments. That will be the Broadway theater, and the misinformation will be complete.

Catch: Other than a direction of total dissolution, do you see serious American theater as having any definite direction?

Albee: Well, it does have a direction, indeed. It continues its investigation of reality, who we are as a society, where we're going, how we think, how we avoid participation. It concerns itself with its fundamental sociopolitical, economic, philosophical, and psychological concerns. It's going about them quite nicely. It's reaching perhaps a smaller or more aware audience and having trouble reaching a larger audience.

Catch: Artistically, are we still in the throes of the depression of the

Nixon administration, or do you see a theatrical renaissance in the future?

Albee: I see such a realignment of serious theater put into small arenas, and away from commercial centers, but I don't know how it will affect things. I suspect it will probably produce two theaters, ultimately completely two. One which is very much like the movies and television, which is junk, escapist junk, and which everybody will go to in great numbers.

Catch: Neil Simon.

Albee: Yeah. And serious theater, which will be subject to economic vicissitudes and small audiences, very probably. That's too bad, because we had, we *had* the opportunity of mixing the two together in a kind of competitive coexistence that was nice.

Catch: You appear to have a distaste for the bulk of criticism being written about your work and about the work of other playwrights. Just how much influence does a critic have on audience response?

Albee: Enormous. The basic problem here being that people who read criticism assume it to be a fact rather than an opinion. If audiences knew that every piece of criticism they read was merely the opinion of somebody, somebody who's not necessarily very bright or very informed, and does not necessarily have the same level of taste as the person who's reading the criticism, then everything would be just fine. I think for so long I was probably fighting the wrong battle, trying to get newspapers and magazines to hire more intelligent and knowledgeable critics. I mean, that's their business. Freedom of the press is in part permitting magazines and newspapers to hire as many imbeciles as they want to be critics. That's called freedom of the press. That's fine. But if people would not read criticism as fact it would help a good deal.

You know, you see people all over the country opening the *New York Times* the morning after a play opens, and saying: "Let's see if the play is any good or not." Well, that's wrong. What they should be opening their paper to say is: "Let's see whether or not Walter Kerr or Frank Rich or Mel Gussow or whoever is reviewing the play, let's see whether or not *he,* to the limits of his intelligence and comprehension, understands and thinks the play is any good." That's what they should be thinking.

Catch: Do you think then that criticism has any validity in the theater?

Albee: I know that if critic A reviews a play that has opened off-Broadway and hates it, I will know that it must be a pretty good play. I will rush to it. If critic B reviews something and likes it, I will know that I will stay away from it.

Catch: Have you ever found a critic that you tended to agree with?

Albee: I find, generally speaking, that critics' sensitivity varies, as it relates to my work, depending on their fondness for it. A certain critic can review one of my plays and be absolutely brilliant about it, and then the next play will turn around and be stupid. You know, won't like it. There are some critics, I think, who can instruct us and tell us something. We lost one of them, named Harold Clurman, quite recently, who was somebody who knew something about the theater, who was a practicing theater man. Though he and I didn't always agree, even about my own work, I found something to respect in most of his attitudes, basically because he was intelligent, also because he knew something about the arts. What bothers me is why so few theater critics are people who know anything about the theater. We don't have that in music. For example, when Virgil Thompson was music critic for the *New York Herald Tribune* and hired as his second-string critics young composers, we had some of the most vital and interesting music criticism in the United States— informed music criticism by people who knew something about music. The best music criticism written now is in *The New Yorker* magazine—Andrew Porter and the fellow that has taken over for him, both trained musicians. I am always more interested in the opinion of people in the arts than I am of people outside the arts. I think we would have an ideal situation if all important critics were people who practiced one of the arts. But they shouldn't necessarily review their *own* art. I think a playwright should be an art critic, a painter should be a critic of poetry, and perhaps a choreographer should review, uh, the novel, and perhaps an essayist the theater. Somebody who is involved in the arts gives a far more perceptive and interesting opinion of the arts for the public point of view than somebody who is this curious thing called a critic, somebody who neither writes nor, quite often, thinks.

Catch: Let me ask one more quick question about the critics and then we'll let them go.

Albee: Are you sure you really want to do that?

Catch: What can criticism do then, to improve the state of the arts, specifically in the theater?

Albee: Shut up.

Catch: And just . . . forget it?

Albee: No. Be informed. Critics have a responsibility to know as much about the art that they write about as the people who practice it do, and if they *don't* know that much they ought to shut up.

Catch: But they have absolutely no right in trying to shape the direction of theater.

Albee: They have no right in trying to shape public opinion or the direction of the theater unless they are equipped to do so, and the trouble with most criticism is that it is written by people who are not equipped.

Catch: *Seascape* was an interesting play for me to read. It seemed to have a sort of optimism—more so than I got from many of your plays. Is this a true perception, and if so, where did it suddenly come from?

Albee: I don't know how optimistic the play is. It's as ambiguous in its ending as any of the others. Does *Who's Afraid of Virginia Woolf?* have a happy ending, for example?

Catch: Does it?

Albee: Are George and Martha going to make it, having leveled the entire structure of their relationship? It's rubble, clear ground. Are they going to be able to build something sensible there? Your guess is as good as mine. I think they have about a fifty-fifty chance of making it—or maybe they won't. I don't know. I don't plan to write *The Son of Who's Afraid of Virginia Woolf?* At the end of *Seascape* we have these two lizard creatures who've continued their evolutionary process to the point where they cannot return to the safety of the sea. They are now going to be subject to *us*, to humanity. Are we going to destroy them? How optimistic is it? I don't know. It depends upon our view of ourselves.

After all, the last line of the play is with the male lizard turning to the human couple who have said, "We will help you," and he says, "All right." It's a threat. I have in my stage direction, very specifically, a threat and a question: "All right. Begin." The implication there is, "If you don't do it right, we'll rip you to pieces." I don't know. That may be a kind of optimism. I'm not sure. But you must remember, optimism is merely writing the work. If I were a pessimist I wouldn't write.

Catch: How's that?

Albee: I mean, if I were an absolute pessimist I would assume that there would be nobody paying any attention, and then why bother?

Catch: Most of your plays deal with a dependence on illusion to make life bearable, perhaps at the expense of a realistic self-appraisal.

Albee: I think this all stems from my experience of O'Neill's play *The Iceman Cometh,* in which he postulated that one had to have this thing called pipe dreams in order to survive. I think most of my works have been an argument against that theory. I think, indeed, one should have false illusions—and probably people *do* need them in order to get through life— but I think they have the responsibility to know that they are kidding themselves and then go right on kidding themselves. That kind of self-awareness is nice.

Catch: So is that the reason you've written plays in this respect?

Albee: Oh, probably. I'm very bad at analyzing what I'm up to. I can give you as much misinformation as any critic can.

Catch: Perhaps some more misinformation from you, then. In some of your works, I get the impression that those human relationships which are most devastating and hurtful are familial, and particularly the marital situation in *Virginia Woolf*. Is this an accurate perception, and if so, why do you think family relationships are this way?

Albee: Well, most people live together in groups of two, three, or four: husband-wife, lovers, two males, two females, whatever you like, uh, children, dogs—there's a small coherent group of people living together, usually. This is the way almost all animals do it. Some animals are monogamous—human beings not among them—some groups of monkeys are monogamous. Other creatures are monogamous. Some birds, curiously enough, are monogamous (you'd think flighty types would not be so monogamous, but they are). Well, we have small, interacting social groups in an intense relationship. This has always been so, and that's why most playwrights have concerned themselves with these small social groups in conflict, starting with Sophocles and Oedipus and his mother, right on down to the present. These are the microcosm that represents the macrocosm. It is something that has concerned almost all playwrights throughout history.

Catch: In particular, though, the family in your work seems to be the bastion of illusion, the place where illusion perhaps is spawned and bred. Is the family, or any small social group, a barrier to realizing the truth?

Albee: It could be used as such, of course. If people use that relationship and that environment as a removal from reality participation, of *course*. James Thurber—who was a far more serious writer than people realize; they think of him as a cartoonist or a humorist when he was a very, very serious writer—uh, wrote in one of his more serious short stories, called *One Is a Wanderer* I believe, that a relationship does not make two people one, a relationship should make two people two, meaning, of course, that it should be a kind of relationship that allows each individual to become himself completely. Most people use relationships as crutches, rather than as growing experiences; they use relationships as a removal from the fray, rather than being able to armor each other for the fray. Most people are using relationships as a retreat rather than a way to engage. That's the problem. No two people who are profoundly in love with each other should be anything but stronger if they were alone, or as strong if they were alone. They must teach each other how to survive as individuals; in that way they can preserve each other as a couple.

Catch: Have you found, in your more recent works, that the individual himself is limiting his potential, regardless of societal restriction whereas, in your earlier work, you saw societal restrictions limiting that potential?

Albee: I may have come to the conclusion that most of the things that I thought were imposed from without are really imposed from within. I suspect so. Yes. Which may be one of the problems with the, uh, critical and public response to some of my more recent plays—that I don't let people off the hook quite so easily.

Catch: You were speaking last night in the lecture about a discussion you had with a Japanese person where he said, "Who are you?" and you were curious as to whether or not that was a Zen question. Did you go ahead and use that in *The Lady from Dubuque*? It seems to me that the whole first half of the second act is essentially a Zen exploration of the question "Who are you?"

Albee: I wouldn't be a bit surprised. I'd never thought of it that way, but I never explore the genesis of anything I do.

Catch: I hadn't thought of it either until you said that last night.

Albee: That, that's a fine point. Maybe that's true. Might be. Might not be. I don't know.

Catch: You're not willing to pin it down.

Albee: As the saying goes, "True if interesting."

Catch: One image that's been repeated in your plays has been the crucifixion image. I got the sense that you use this image—in *The Zoo Story*, in fact—to represent something.

Albee: I wouldn't be a bit surprised. I was raised in something bordering upon a religion. I was raised in the Episcopal Church. Which I left when I was five, uh, having outgrown it, I think. I would imagine there is a lot of the Christian mythology that enters into my work. Also, I've always been very interested in Jesus Christ. I think he's an extraordinary individual. And I wouldn't be a bit surprised that, uh, . . . I would love some day, I suspect, to write a play about him. I doubt if I'll ever do it—very specifically about him. But it is, I think, a deeply held . . . love affair that I have with the man. . . . Don't tell *him*.

I think it interesting that after I wrote *The Zoo Story*, I received a letter from a very nice nun in Brooklyn pointing out that *The Zoo Story* was chock full of Christian symbolism—that Peter and Jerry were close to Peter and Jesus, and that Peter denies three times that he knows what Jerry is talking about. And though I hadn't *consciously* put all those things in the play I wasn't surprised to read about them.

Catch: You did not consciously put Peter's denial in the play three times? I really thought you had.

Albee: No. No. But once, of course, it was pointed out to me that I had, then obviously I had done it on purpose.

Catch: It was such a clever idea.

Albee: That's, uh, that's what you do with the things that people tell you you've done. If they make you seem far more interesting than you consciously *were,* you incorporate those things as part of your original intention. Naturally. This based on the assumption that nobody can find anything of value or of great interest in the work unless the author put it there whether he was consciously aware of putting it there or not. Nothing can be found that is not there.

Catch: You've mentioned O'Neill's *The Iceman Cometh.* I was wondering if you could tell us what other playwrights have influenced you.

Albee: Well, that's difficult because I have certain favorites among playwrights—like Chekhov and Beckett, for example—but how much have they influenced me? I hope enormously, but I hope it's not evident. And there are some plays that I think very specifically influenced me that I don't necessarily admire a great deal. I don't think of *The Iceman Cometh* as a totally successful play, but I think it probably had a profound influence on me. I don't think that Tennessee Williams's *Suddenly Last Summer* is necessarily a completely successful play, though a pretty good one—and I think *that* had a considerable influence on me. But I'm influenced by everything I experience. Somebody once asked me what playwrights influenced me, and I heard myself reply, "Sophocles and Noël Coward," because it's *true.* There is something to be gotten from both of them. You should always be influenced not only by what's very, very good but also by what's bad. From what's very, very good you learn what to do, and from something that fails you learn what not to do. And so people who go around reading only masterpieces aren't learning their craft.

Catch: What do you think it was about your work that made you emerge from the pack of playwrights of which you were a member in the early sixties?

Albee: I don't know. I kept writing and the others didn't, very much. Jack Richardson declined into gambling. Arthur Kopit writes a play about every eight years, now. Jack Gelber writes a few of them, but they don't seem to be very popular—he writes a play about every four or five years. I have had the tenacity of going right on writing a play a year. Uh. LeRoi Jones—who is no longer LeRoi Jones, is now Imamu Amiri Baraka—has given up art for dialectic, and has destroyed himself and his creative force, unfortunately. That was the first bunch of us. Some of the ones who came along a few years later are still working. I don't know, some of us have a certain tenacity, a certain staying power, others don't.

Catch: I think I have one last question. Um. This, in fact, largely because we asked a similar question of novelist Vance Bourjaily last spring term. It had often been stated that American novelists—and I think this can be twisted and pointed toward playwrights as well by those people who would have stated it—that American novelists were incapable of writing a strong female character. They always came off as either bitches or goddesses. Do you think this has any validity, and if it did for novelists, would it have any for playwrights?

Albee: Well, you've got to start, here, from the understanding that most serious plays are not written about well-adjusted people getting along well with each other. Most serious plays are written about people *not* getting along with each other—with the exception of *Oedipus Rex,* where everybody was getting along too well, perhaps—uh, they are about people in disarray. You can't *do* a dramatic act about a well-adjusted couple sitting around being very happy. There is absolutely no dramatic conflict. You can't do it. And you examine the ladies in literature . . . Is Clytemnestra *fun*? Were Lear's daughters nice to have around? Wasn't Hedda Gabler a rather awful person? It is the nature of drama.

Catch: So you think this is an inappropriate criticism to be brought even against novelists?

Albee: Oh, certainly. Of course. Indeed, yes. I mean, we write our plays and we write our novels to say to people, "Look, this is the way you are. You don't like it? Oh! Well, then why don't you change it?"

Catch: Is the primary purpose of art to teach?

Albee: I suppose, ultimately, it is. To make people more aware of themselves, which is a teaching experience.

MIA WESTERLUND ROOSEN

1982

IN JANUARY OF this year in New York, two of the most established Fifty-seventh Street galleries mounted a joint exhibit—same artists in both galleries; works from the forties in one, recent pieces in the other. It wasn't a profoundly interesting show: not all the artists were first or even second rate, nor were the examples chosen of the better artists always of a high quality.

Still, the show was provocative in that it focused on two matters vital to a comprehensive consideration of the worth of any artist—continuity and growth. Some of the artists in the double show do the same work now they did thirty years ago; with some, the present pieces come from a different land than the earlier; with most, however, the same mind and hand are clearly there as the artists grow or decline over the decades.

We have all watched as artists climb the rungs and reach that awful plateau on which critical and art buying public acceptance married to a powerhouse dealer produce in them a decade of stasis wherein they produce the same rapidly snapped-up piece over and over again. Just as sadly we have watched an artist flounder—more from one manner to another—in search of either his own "true nature" or, perhaps, one nicely resonant to the present public aesthetic.

What we look for, then, with greatest enthusiasm, is the artist who follows his own aesthetic nose—unself-conscious but not unself-aware—and whose next inevitable step is always surprising until hindsight makes it all clear to us.

John Duff and Mia Westerlund Roosen strike me as being two sculptors who follow these proper precepts, and, it is Westerlund who concerns us here.

Her work of the last ten years, leading up to and culminating in the present show at Leo Castelli (Greene Street), shows an almost dizzying progress of matter and manner, yet an overseeing aesthetic governs the journey from bandages of fiber and resin wrapped around tubes of air, through giant paving stones of incised concrete; through megaliths of copper and concrete rising as startlingly yet surely as the previous slabs stay put; through unexpected concrete and steel shapes wrapped, sheathed, or entwined in lead or wax, to the present garden of unearthly delights.

One looks in vain for the tentative intellectual or emotional gesture in Westerlund's work. Her commitment to each (to us) unexpected shift—from horizontal to vertical, from angles to their absence, from geometry to a kind of anthropomorphism—is complete and sure. The laurels are there in each seemingly precipitous step she takes, but she is unwilling to rest on them for any length of time. Occasionally, this impatience makes us long for a fuller mining of each aesthetic lode, for we know there are untouched riches—depths—which persistence would uncover, but then we are gathered up in the impetus of her newest thrust, and we find the departure both exhilarating and instructive.

No exhibit of Westerlund's work is less than provocative and the present one may be the most challenging yet—both for her band of admirers and your average off-the-street culture clutcher.

The enormous drawings accompanying the sculpture—alternately dense and airy, all very specifically "sculptor's drawings" and not studies for the pieces—offer fewer problems for either the cognoscente or their (perhaps) happier brethren. The drawings are about themselves, about how one sculptor thinks on paper.

Some of the sculpture, on the other hand, is bound to cause referential difficulty—has already!—for those who insist on seeing what an abstract piece "looks like" rather than what it "is." Indeed, one of the smaller horizontal pieces can be read as feces, and another of the reclining works can easily be seen as penile— if that is how one wishes to read and see. There is a fascinating mutuality in an artist's responsibility to take the viewer's eye and mind beyond referential experience, and the viewer's willingness to be thus led, one which is perhaps not unintentionally examined here—a daring.

Some of the pieces are cool and elegant; some are exuberantly ugly; all seem to have existed where they sit—wherever they sit— forever. They are truly prehistoric, and if there is a collective unconscious, then that is their domain.

While Westerlund's fascination with materials for their own sake remains constant—her concrete calls attention to its composition, its surfaces; her wax comments on the ways of wax—she has moved, over the past ten years, away from her own version of "process art," with its predeterminations, its ultimate limitings, to a freer kind of modeling.

She writes: "After a certain point the high importance of process proved to be too restrictive on my work. Therefore I made a basic philosophical shift in my method of making sculpture. It is still necessary to have a general shape in mind at the core of the piece (for instance: a cone), but through the manipulation of the material an unpredetermined shape becomes the focal issue. In other words, keeping the integrity of the material and the handling of it in the forefront, the step has been toward a redefinition of 'modeling.' The piece is ultimately free to take on any shape. The actual rendering of the shape is therefore much slower with individual decisions being made constantly. To a certain extent, the manipulation of the material can be considered the source of meaning. But, ultimately, the sculpture is the expression of an inwardly oriented consciousness manifesting itself in a three-dimensional object in space."

And on top of all that, the new work is adventuresome, perverse, assured, and provocative.

Informed Joy

1988

I CRINGE WHENEVER I hear the term "art collector," both for perhaps unjustified associative suggestion—garbage collector, injustice collector—and for the sad awareness that most art collections—except the infrequent truly significant ones—are either embarrassingly trendy, riddled with third-rate works by famous artists, or are the accumulation of works chosen not by the (perhaps) recently affluent "collector," but by a hired hand presumably knowledgeable in the area the "collector" wishes to be known for.

There are, of course, extraordinary collections of extraordinary art, thoughtful, provocative, responsible teaching instruments, gathered by knowledgeable, sophisticated individuals, most of whom are aware they are accumulating as a public trust. These, however, are the exceptions. And it is only *they* who deserve being called "collections."

The rest of us, those of us who have, over a period of many years, accumulated art objects of some beauty and provocation and are guilty of neither vanity nor artistic ignorance do not think of ourselves as "collectors"; we are disturbed by the word. We are—what?—"accumulators"? I suppose. We have accumulated— I have, at any rate—because we are comforted and stimulated, surrounded by the beautiful and the provocative.

People often seem surprised that I—a writer—am deeply interested in the visual arts. If they thought more about how a playwright works—that the eye and the ear are more fundamental to our craft than they are to a novelist or a poet—they would not be so surprised. A playwright puts down on the page what is to be seen and heard—either on the stage or in the eye and ear of the receiving mind. Playwrights are highly visual folk; we must—if we are to be any good—hear time like a composer and see space like a painter or a sculptor. Therefore, it does not surprise me that I tried to be both a composer and a painter in my teens—was better, but not much, at the second than the first—and have now an encyclopedic knowledge of classical music and an assemblage of between three and four hundred art objects.

The assemblage is heavily weighted toward twentieth-century painting, sculpture and drawing (two thirds of it U.S.), a sprinkling of antiquities, and perhaps fifty pieces of folk art—African, pre-Columbian, Mexican, and Oceanic for the most part.

Not being a wealthy man I have never collected for profit; though, having an informed eye I have watched some acquisitions appreciate hundreds of times their original value (or, purchase price, to be more accurate) over the years. And, on the other hand, since I enjoy encouraging young artists—buying early, early work—I have been occasionally disappointed to see a promising career go nowhere.

If I were to define my motivation as an art accumulator it would be . . . informed joy.

"I don't know anything about art, but I know what I like," says the art imbecile.

"I know everything about art, but I temper my enthusiasms; what I like is less important than what I *should* like," says the art investor.

* * *

I dearly hope my time in the art world has avoided the extremes above. I think I know what I'm doing, and my budget limitations have saved me from the prudence required for "major acquisition."

I have chosen the fifteen works in this exhibition to represent some of my recent enthusiasms among younger and less well-known artists. (You will notice that I have included eighty-five-year-old Maud Morgan among "younger" artists.) All of the work has been acquired in the past five years; five of the artists are foreign—Czechoslovakia, Japan, Great Britain, Canada—and ten from the United States. The U.S. artists hover around thirty years of age, while the non-U.S. artists tend to be in their forties. Five of the artists have been residents at the William Flanagan Memorial Creative Persons Center, an activity of the Edward F. Albee Foundation, Inc., located in Montauk, on Long Island, and providing studio and living space for some twenty-five writers, composers, and visual artists each summer.

The average cost of the art works at time of acquisition was $1,500.

It Is the Dark We Have to Fear

1989

I'M GLAD TO be a playwright—which is fortunate, since it is what I am (it's nice to be able to practice one's nature). I thoroughly enjoy the fact that the creative act is constantly at war with the status quo. But our proper function as creative artists is being corrupted by a devastating misunderstanding of the purpose of the arts in our society today.

In a democracy—as I understand it—people are permitted to go their own way, enjoy themselves as they prefer, vote as shortsightedly as they desire, and pass their lives as fully involved or as emptily as they wish, so long as they don't frighten the horses and so long as they pay reasonable attention to the "common good," as phrased in law. The "common good," however, is more complex a matter than what is merely legal. The "common good" has to do with consciousness—the one thing beyond the absence of a tail that differentiates us from the other animals. And the choices that a society makes about self-education—civil, moral, and aesthetic self-education—determine its grasp on the wonders and perils of awareness, of consciousness.

Examine for a moment the function of art in a democratic society—especially since in a democratic society there is, or should be, no intentional governmental control of the free expression of the arts. The function of the arts is to hold a mirror up to people, to say, "This is how you are. Take a hard look; if you don't like what you see, change." The function of the arts is to bring order out of chaos, coherence out of the endless static, the gibberish of the stars, and to render people capable of thinking metaphorically. The arts are an essential part of public education, and without their special lucidity, the college graduate is only half a conscious soul.

I dare say it is useless, as things are presently set up, to expect the marriage of art and commerce in a free-wheeling capitalist society to produce anything other than mediocrity at best. The short-term stakes are too high. "Sell the people what they want. To hell with values; business runs on profit." The function of art is to bring people into greater touch with reality, and yet our movie houses and family rooms are jammed with people after as much reality-removal as they can get. Our commercial theaters are filled with people eager for the spectacle of mindless junk, while the serious plays—those that can tell us something about both ourselves and the practice of serious theater as an art form—are to be found, in the main, in small theaters built for small audiences. The most popular books, the most popular music, the most popular television teach us nothing about what it is to be a reasoning, conscious animal.

You know as well as I that those responsible for the point of view of the television networks, the movie companies, the publishing

houses, and the newspapers and magazines of this land are determined that a badly informed public is best served by the absence
of choice. "Don't rock the boat." The arts criticism of our most
important communications outlets is carefully modulated to
create a safe, middle-brow, upper-echelon mediocrity as the
standard—a stale environment, where the adventurous, the
thrilling, the joyous, and the dangerous are seen as the enemy.

Many of you will remember Walter Kerr, a rather famous
drama critic in the United States—and not a bad one. Walter Kerr
was a well-educated man (educated at the skirts of the Jesuits), a
man whose aesthetic could be trusted (though perhaps not beyond
the first third of the twentieth century), a bright man, an enormously powerful critic for the late, lamented *Herald Tribune* and
for the *New York Times,* and one of the most influential theater
critics we have had in this country. Kerr once made a remark on
public television that I believe is the essence of what I am trying
to point out today. He said, "I consider it my function as a critic
to reflect what I consider to be the taste of the readers of the newspaper for which I work." Here was a man creating public taste,
defining aesthetic consciousness for an entire society—and considering it his responsibility to "reflect" the public taste. The
public looks to the Walter Kerrs of the present day for instruction,
for guidance, and all they are seeing is the reflection of their own
misjudgment of the function of art.

In a democracy you cannot stop public access to that art that
will most misinform the people. You cannot stop people from
being misinformed. But what you can do is to educate the people
to the point that they will throw the rascals out. I know, for
example, that if I were given all the money on Broadway and all
of its theaters to show only the finest plays of world literature for

twenty years, at the end of those twenty years those plays would represent the theater taste of our society. The American public is not hopeless; the American public is *helpless*. I also know . . . that no one knows as much about what is useful, instructive, and valuable in the arts as does the creative artist. In my thirty-year career as a playwright, I have never learned as much from any critic or lay-audience member about the practice of my craft as I have learned from my fellow creative artists. What I have learned from critics and lay audiences is how long my plays will *run*. But what I have learned from my fellow creative artists is how long my plays will *matter*.

I would like to put these two points together. Public and private arts support organizations are capable of bringing together, far more even than they are doing now, the aesthetic education of a free society and those who can teach the best—the creative artists themselves. . . .

It is not enough to fill your juries, your advisory panels, with creative artists. You must put us in positions of policy control. The danger is simple, and it is this: unless you are terribly, terribly careful, you run the danger—without even knowing it is happening to you—of slipping into the fatal error of reflecting the public taste instead of creating it. Your responsibility is to the public consciousness, not to the public view of itself. The pressures on you must be considerable, but there *are* absolutes in this world. And the historical continuum of the arts shows us that there are absolutes of value in the arts. Public fashion, critical reading of public desire, economic balance sheets, will not aid you in knowing these absolutes and responding properly to them. Creative artists *will* know.

It is not enough to hold the line against the dark. It is your responsibility to lead into the light. People don't like the light—it reveals too much. But hand in hand with the creative artist, you can lead people into the wisdom that is known to all other animals: simply, that it is the dark we have to fear.

LEE KRASNER

1990

EVEN A FEW years ago it was a far more complex matter to write about Lee Krasner's art than it is now. Back then there was so much extra-art garbage surrounding her work that it was an effort to move into the pure center and experience the painting for its own sake.

The two piles of garbage—towers, actually—were made up of ignorance and careerism, both topped by a mould of half-truth and superstition. These piles of garbage were named "female artist" and "wife of artist." You can still see mounds such as these in the more intellectually backward areas of the United States.

The notion that women are less aesthetically profound and innovative than men—just not very important, if you know what I mean—doubtless spreads back to our beginnings as upright animals: the males hunted and killed for the family while the females stayed home in the cave and tended the strange little creatures they were giving birth to.

The theory evolved: men provide, women stay home, cook, and

rear. It seems to have evolved further: men see and represent what they see as art; women stay home, cook, and rear. It is a theory which began to break down seriously only in this century, and slowly even then; nor has it vanished with all the other pre-Copernican, pre-Gallilean nonsense.

(In passing, I wonder who *really* painted the walls at Lascaux. *Was* it a hunter home from the hill, or was it the first female reporter, skulking after the men, observing them, then hurrying back to the cave where the dyes were already mixed—women's work, of course—eager to record the outside events for the stay-at-homes?)

I suppose there are women art critics who are negatively sexist even today, just as there are women art critics who see virtue only in a skirt—guerrilla girls for the Guerrilla Girls, so to speak; they join the men who refuse to accept that women artists can bend and shape our aesthetic perceptions.

The women writers of the world have it better; the work of Anna Akhmatova and Nadezhda Mandelstam may well be the finest Russian writing since Chekhov; Marguerite Duras and Nathalie Sarraute are equal to the best of the postwar male French avant-guardists; Nadine Gordimer and Doris Lessing are doubt-less Nobel Prize candidates; and here at home we have so many splendid women writers—Cynthia Ozick and Susan Sontag, to name but two—that one day I expect our publishing houses to be run in tandem by men and women.

But in the visual arts the scene for women has been tougher. While it is true that Goncharova's reputation didn't suffer much when it was discovered that she was a woman, I suspect that a lot of art writers and tastemakers would have been happier had she not been. While it is true that Nevelson's work is generally granted master status, the build of her reputation was greatly swiftened by her making herself a household name through shrewd self-promotion. And it is shocking to me that Louise Bourgeois, who showed her genius in the 1940s has only in the past few years—and even grudgingly—been accorded her due.

The situation may be beginning to change, but there is not a woman artist I can think of now who, manner for manner, generation for generation, accomplishment for accomplishment has received the critical acceptance, financial reward, or impingement on the public consciousness of her male counterparts.

I will brook no interference when I assert that Lee Krasner is not only the finest woman painter the United States has produced in this century but—since sex is really not the vital matter here—is right in the top of the pile of great twentieth-century American artists, period.

Her ascent was hampered by two considerations: she was a woman, and she was the wife of a great painter. "Woman" we have covered, but "Mate to the Great" we have not. How could Lee Krasner be taken seriously, the line ran, when she was the wife of Jackson Pollock, watched him at work, and doubtless learned and copied, learned and copied? This maddening sexist claptrap was unavoidable if preposterous. It has afflicted other artistic closenesses; for example, Barbara Hepworth's reputation suffered after her relationship with Henry Moore ended, after they had had cross-fertilized each other's aesthetic profoundly in the thirties.

A close examination of Krasner and Pollock paintings of the period they lived and worked together shows great mutual influence, of course, and great individuality, as well. While I would not deny the burgeoning of Krasner's work after Pollock's death in 1956 (a freeing from all the womanly concerns, perhaps?), an examination of her art in totality—the huge Houston retrospective of 1983, for example—shows the straight line of artistic maturing toward inevitability joined to a remarkable technical assurance right from the very beginning. There is no marriage blip there. The work was its own from the start and merely grew in self-awareness.

No one who knew Lee Krasner either casually or as well as I did can deny that her personality may have given comfort and ammunition to those who were unwilling to grant her her artistic due. She had an enemies list as comprehensive as Nixon's, though perhaps with greater cause; hers was constructed far more of vengeance than of paranoia. She suffered fools—and others—less gladly than most people I have known, but her friendships were as profound as her justified loathings. I adored her and think she liked me, as well.

What strikes me most about these paintings of the middle and late sixties is their exuberance. To the cyclical continuity of her work—it is all of one piece, ultimately, from the post-cubist student drawings, through the John Graham–like early paintings, through the extraordinary torn strip "rejection" pieces, through it all—she seems to have added one element . . . pure joy. These paintings dance and prance and sweep and swerve and shout in their enthusiasm. All is exuberance—the great arcs of paint, the astonishing juxtapositions of color. It is not a mindless outpouring, of course—intellectual control is behind the free spirit in every canvas. What it is, most precisely, is the joyous outpouring of a major artist who is sure of her gift and is happy to share it.

JOHN DUFF

1990

SCULPTURE CREATES PROBLEMS for the collector, doesn't it?
Sculpture tends to be bulky; it tends to be heavy; it tends to be
very three-dimensional; at its best—just like painting—it tends to
be very "serious"; some of it tends to be happy only outdoors, and
even when it is content to be indoors it calls attention to itself in
disturbing ways painting does not often do; it tends—again at its
very best—to be nondecorative and intrusive (or is assertive a
politer term?); very little of it tends to relate to a decor—"build
around *me*!" it seems to say; and—this is far too important to far
too many—its "art market movement" tends to be sluggish—far
less sculpture is bought as investment, or commodity, than is
painting.

Sculpture also creates problems for its creators. It tends to be
bulky; it tends to be heavy; it tends to cost the artist a lot more
money to make than it does a painter a painting; collectors tend
to be less eager to accumulate it than they do paintings; therefore
dealers tend to be less eager to show it than they are paintings.

(Though, of course, if more dealers showed sculpture more collectors would buy it.)

But—in the end—one is what one is: one is a dealer; one is a collector; one is a sculptor. That which we do is an extension of that which we are and sculptors are stuck with it—stuck with the bulky, the heavy, the three-dimensional, the "serious," the nondecorative, the intrusive, the not-so-immediately saleable. Good for them!

We are what we do, and we are most what we do best. It is interesting to note in passing, though, that while a number of first-rate twentieth-century painters have made sizeable contributions to sculpture, very few sculptors have added much to our comprehension of painting.

Matisse and Picasso come to mind immediately, as do Rauschenberg and Stella—though it may be said (except by him) that Stella has become a sculptor (and, to the minds of many, a less provocative artist), and that Rauschenberg has always been both. Looking at some of our first-rate twentieth-century sculptors—Brancusi, González, Giacometti, Bourgeois, Noguchi, for example—we see little in their flat work of comparative provocation. Oh, most sculptors—many, anyway—do interesting drawings, and, while Giacometti's paintings and drawings are lovely to see they are, ultimately, thoughts about three-dimensional space, thoughts about sculpture, and Bourgeois's hermetic drawings give us some slantwise access to her overall metaphor; still, the parallels do not draw.

Most painters do not sculpt; most sculptors do not paint. When painters sculpt they tend to be more useful than are sculptors when they paint.

Does this teach us anything? Well, yes; probably that sculptors think of what they do more as "thing" than as "art"—note the quotes about both words; that important sculpture, given its three-dimensionality, its "thingness," alters not only how we see but how we sense; that sculptors think differently than painters in that they deal with the real rather than the illusory, and that the metaphor flows less indirectly from the artwork created to the perceptor than it inevitably does in painting.

Much the same as in theater, a play is a representation of an event, while a film is a representation of a representation, a sculpture does not demand the extra artifice. Nothing pejorative is intended here, of course: all art is artifice; it is this artifice, this metaphorical distancing which gives art its reality, its power.

There are quite a few of us who feel that sculpture these days is more provocative than painting as a general rule (see Germany and Japan as cases in point), that it is telling us more interesting things about how to look at art and how to think about what we look at. Certainly the middle generation of U.S. sculptors—Duff, Puryear, Westerlund Roosen, Shapiro, Nonas, as example—is doing work of both vitality and serenity, orneriness and classic purity, intellectual rigor and emotional expansiveness. What unites them—for all their differences, their individualities—is the awareness that sculpture can be many things that painting cannot, should not, and that sculpture can be fresher—newer, less explored, if you will—than the other, and, most certainly, less exploited.

I have known John Duff's work for over twenty years, have watched it move from its detritus-oriented beginnings, through the early geometric fiberglass wall pieces, through the intriguing metal rod "drawings in space," through the bronze pottery—harking back to his *very* beginnings, through the return to fiberglass, now more freely shaped and lusciously colored, through the bronze table and floor pieces of a few years ago (helixes, etc.), to the present exhibit.

Across the years the work has been constantly stimulating, the shifts the inevitable consequence of a restless, fertile mind interested in the limits of craft and art. The present exhibit seems to me to be Duff's most provocative yet. The sources which have always moved him—the organic, the primitive, the mathematical, the scientific, the "unheard-of"—are joined here to stunning effect. Some of the pieces hum, or vibrate, or pulse (not literally, of course); some are eerily, steely silent; the colors seem to inhabit the shapes, to have always inhabited them; the shapes themselves seem to have always existed—once we experience them, that is; that we are surprised by them means merely that we have not imagined them.

All of the paradoxes essential to the finest art are present: clarity and ambiguity, presence and remoteness, expectation and confounding. It is sculpture and nothing else—pure and not so simple. It is Duff's most mature and satisfying work, a coming together of so many ideas. It is rare for so many promises to be kept all at once.

ROBERT JUAREZ

1990

MANY YEARS AGO when I first lived in New York City and began to move around in the creative world—not yet as a contributor but as a very quiet learning observer, absorber—I was struck by how coherent a community it *was*—a group of artists, writers, composers working their minds off (often only for the benefit of each other) with great seriousness and dedication, with enormous hope if not with much rational expectation.

Oh, there were hustlers even then, of course, manipulators, those who sensed that a big game was forming, that the brass ring—like some grail—was brightening in the murk, and probably there were a few of us who knew who they were and what they were up to in that compact, unself-conscious environment, but there was no haste among the rest of us, merely engagement, no teeth-grinding career anxiety, merely self-assurance and persistence.

The composers gathered at the Carnegie Tavern, the painters at the Cedar Street, the writers et cetera at the San Remo and the Caffe Cino. It was a community within a city of seven million; we all knew one another, and seldom were brows knit in career planning, eyes narrowed in suspicion. Were we naive, or merely deeply engaged? I'm not sure. Nonetheless, it was a complete world . . . and then it all fell apart.

Overnight—it seemed—our innocence was gone; the arts had become big business; careers were manufactured rather than being allowed to evolve. More destructively, the concept of the arts as commodity upset the proper hierarchy and constructed a system in which the buyer . . . formerly the grateful recipient—in tandem with ambitious critics and shrewd middlemen (dealers, publishers, producers, whatever) became king, and the creator became an artisan, scrambling to satisfy the not necessarily sophisticated taste of the purchaser.

The you-know-what hit the fan, and when the stuff was scraped off the blades it looked and smelled suspiciously like money.

Now, very few creative artists like being poor, and popularity is probably preferable to obscurity, and power and fame are a swell fix, and now and again the buyers, the critics, and the middlemen have proved to be right (though usually long after the creative community has known where the absolute value sits), but there is this Faust thing running around, and too many souls have been bought or sold in the world of the arts in the past twenty-or-so years to make one particularly comfortable about the public aesthetic of this country.

I visit the studios of young painters and sculptors with some frequency, and I have noticed (noticed, indeed!!, have had forced on my consciousness) far too many of them sitting blankly, not waiting for inspiration to strike but for an answer to the great mystery . . . "which way is the bandwagon heading now?"

These are bright folks; they know that one does not climb on the passing vehicle, that that scramble is for the third rate. No, they sit and ponder which way the bandwagon might be coming and once they have figured *that* out, they go to work to be there when it arrives. How do they do this?—throw dice? ponder the course of art history? buy dinner for a few critics who . . . ? examine the entrails of sitting ducks? Any or all of the above are equally helpful in avoiding the only course that matters: mastering the past and inventing the future.

Of course, there are a lot of bright, very gifted young artists at work out there who hear their own drummer and understand the need to march only to it. Robert Juarez is one of these. His mastery of his materials is most impressive; clearly he has understood the conscious and unconscious aims of his precursors, and equally clearly he has stared at his own navel with essential accepting self-absorption.

The newest paintings—the "Days of the Year" series—surprised him, Juarez says, by which he means (I am certain) that he thought about them considerably without being aware of it and then had the courage to let them come into being without second-guessing them, guided only by his eye, his hand and—in a very non-sectarian sense of it—his faith.

This not a con artist at work; the paintings are not slick, nor are they glib. They are achievements of a man who knows his craft, who knows his art, and who knows his mind.

"INSTINCTIVE TINGLE"

1990

Judy Collischan Van Wagner interviews Edward Albee.

Q: How long have you been collecting?

A: I don't know that I ever have, because I don't like the term. Accumulating?

   I wanted to be a painter when I was very young, but was terrible, so I quit it. I've always been interested in the visual arts even when I was going to school. I bought my first painting then, and I still have it.

Q: When was that?

A: 1960. I got thrown out of school. When *The Zoo Story* opened, I quit my job with Western Union and started looking out for paintings.

Q: And you still look here in New York and as you travel.

A: Not only in artists' studios, but also in galleries and museums. I find things everywhere. Not only contemporary paintings, but historical and primitive work.

Q: Why have you kept on collecting?

A: I think it's much more interesting if you have a few dollars to put them on your walls rather than in a bank.

Q: The different types of art that you collect—historical painting, sculpture, African and Oriental art, do you find relationships among them? Do you use the same criteria of judgment?

A: To me all art is useful. In primitive societies they didn't distinguish between utility and art. I don't think we should either.

Q: How would you define the function of art in a primitive culture as opposed to our own?

A: Well, ultimately, if you use my standards, there is no difference. But unfortunately, most people don't use my standards so there is a difference. All art in primitive societies was utilitarian. It was there for religious purposes fundamentally, or mythic purposes in one sense or another. There was no distinction made between utility and fine art. That was one of the most interesting things about it. We have created this thing called "Fine Art," and most people think that it lacks utility, but goodness, go back to Greek sculpture—that was highly utilitarian. Renaissance painting, enormously utilitarian—for religious purposes. All great art is utilitarian, but we've made this distinction so that fine arts quite often seem merely decorative. That's a great shame.

Q: To you, that's an artificial distinction.

A: I do think that's a very artificial distinction, because great art should tell us something more about ourselves in relation to the rest of the world. When Cézanne first painted a blue tree, it changed the way our eyes worked.

Q: In what way?

A: We'd never seen that trees were blue before.

Q: Did you study painting at any point?

A: I didn't study anything in school. I don't believe in studying stuff. If you have a fairly good mind and some enthusiasm, you can learn by yourself.

   You should be able to relate all of the arts, one to the other. You can find a kind of relationship if you don't isolate yourself with painting but are aware of what's going on in other art forms.

Q: Is there a particular relationship between theater and visual art?

A: All art is useful, if it's any good at all. It has to be socially useful. Anything that is merely decorative has absolutely no use at all. Anytime I go to the theater, I feel my time has been wasted unless it has extended the boundaries of my theatrical experience and made me rethink my values. Whenever I look at a painting, I want it to change the possibilities of the art form for me. I want it to expand art in some way that is highly moral because it makes us reevaluate it. If it just lies there and is pretty, it's socially corrupt. Art should make some comment on how one views consciousness. It should make me think differently about consciousness and the art form itself—both.

Q: By consciousness, do you mean social consciousness?

A: Social involvement, yes. Involvement with one's own life on this planet, one's participation in one's own life.

Q: As a playwright and teacher of playwrighting, then you feel that a play should have a socially useful function?

A: A play should examine how we think about things. There's no point in leaving us the way we were. Make us think. Shake us up. Make us examine what we believe, and see if we really believe it. Make us look at things that maybe we don't want to look at because they're tough to look at. In other words make us participate in our living more fully.

Q: You don't necessarily mean to shock people.

A: No, sometimes you can be nice and insidious, come up from behind and club them over the head without their knowing it's happening. Some of the most serious drama has been comedy. Let's not forget Aristophanes, for example, who was every bit as interesting as Sophocles. Let's not forget Molière or Chekhov. Let's not forget Beckett—an enormously funny playwright. Oscar Wilde was a great social critic and an enormously funny writer. So was Sean O'Casey, come to think of it.

Q: What will eventually happen to the Albee collection?

A: I'll give it all to the Edward F. Albee Foundation, the function of which is to supply the wherewithal for artists to work. I want this art to either be kept or sold to aid young artists.

Q: When was the Foundation begun?

A: About twenty-two years ago. We have twenty-four artists a year of which six are visual artists. The others are writers and composers, some of whom have made considerable careers for themselves.

Q: So the Foundation is sort of your philosophy of relating the arts in action?

A: Yes.

Q: Do the visual and performing arts influence your art form?

A: I'm an instinctive playwright, and I don't like to examine my art too carefully. But I suppose it has because I've been constantly involved in the visual arts and in listening to classical music since I was very young. Being a playwright where I use both my eye and my ear, I think it's pretty useful or helpful that I have been involved in both the visual and auditory arts as long as I have.

Q: What advice would you give to potential art collectors?

A: If you're going to be a serious collector, you should never collect with the idea of resale. Actually, I see no point in collecting at all unless you have what I call "informed taste." Know something about the art that interests you. Know its history and its commerce. For example, if you like one artist, don't buy third-rate examples of his work just to acquire the name. You don't buy reproductions or cheap prints of an artist; you buy original works and the very best works you can. Never even think about collecting an artist because you think or somebody told you, "Oh, this one's going to be big and you're going to make a lot of money." The only way you can really ever make a lot of money or if you're interested in having a valuable collection is to have really good informed taste.

Q: How does one train their eye?

A: I don't know that there are any rules to it. That's why so many of what are referred to as major collectors these days have someone with informed taste collecting for them. These people have money but not informed taste, so they hire their own private curators to buy work for them.

Q: Can one learn by looking a lot, by spending time looking at art?

A: There are some people who can look their whole lives and are never going to know the difference between a good and a terrible piece of art, while there are some who get an instinctive tingle over something wonderful. If you have informed taste, you've got to trust your own judgment. You have to need and love something before you get it, not just because, "Oh, that might be nice," or "It goes with the sofa." It must be something you feel a personal involvement with. That's terribly important.

Unless you have a great deal of money, I think you should collect younger artists. Older established artists—the prices are through the ceiling now, and nobody can afford them. Take chances with younger artists, with primitive art, with African, Oceanic, or Pre-Columbian art, but again, know what you're doing. Go only to reputable dealers, because there are a lot of charlatans in the world.

Q: Could you describe the state of art today, in this country and in New York City?

A: I find that middlebrowism is rampant. Generally speaking, I find that truly high art has a harder time than it had maybe twenty-five years ago, because people want stuff that's a little safer. But we probably have more access to all of the arts in this country per square foot than any other society has, if people will merely pay attention to it.

Q: What about censorship?

A: We do have to worry a great deal about arts censorship in this country—the Jesse Helms of this world and those people who would wish to take away our freedom of creative expression. The obscenity that Jesse Helms objects to, I find basically existing in his attitudes.

Q: Is there too much commercialism involved in today's art world?

A: I think it's misleading a great many people, yes. And I think it's disturbing a number of artists who can no longer work with the tranquility they had before art became big business. I see too many young artists desperately worried these days about, "Is what I'm doing going to be popular? Is it going to sell? Will my career be made by this, by that?" They're concerned about these questions rather than going on the way they used to—twenty or thirty years just painting. I find that the commercial aspects of the art world have corrupted a lot of artists.

Q: Are people misled in terms of "hype" given to certain artists?

A: Oh sure. But everybody wants to catch the brass ring, you see. Everybody wants to get on the merry-go-round.

Q: What is the alternative to a commercial system?

A: The alternative is to have an educated public. I've always thought that a public education is incomplete unless it includes aesthetic education. We have only half-educated kids in this country by guaranteeing completion of the twelfth grade in high school, but ignoring aesthetic education. A civilized person is an esthetically informed and educated one who is able to choose between good and bad, moral and evil. I'm delighted to see hordes of second and third graders going through a museum, even if it's not always for the right reasons—getting them out of the classroom. But these kids are being exposed to art and that's wonderful.

Q: Are museums doing their job today in terms of showing art?

A: So much of what is going on in today's museums is not valuable, and it's not interesting. It has to do with what's trendy and fashionable and what the fancy people are attracted to. I don't think it's a museum's responsibility to keep up with that awful kind of glitz-trendiness. It's the intelligent curator's responsibility to have a sense of what's really going on in the world as opposed to the glitz.

Q: In spite of the glitz, is it important for artists to live in or experience Manhattan?

A: A playwright who lives thousands of miles from any theater is at an impossible disadvantage. Unless the playwright can understand the relationship between the play on the stage and the form of the play, how theater works and what it looks like, he's not ever going to become a theater person. One of the interesting things about art, particularly abstract art as it is practiced in the Soviet Union, is that it is made without the physical experience of influences. These artists only saw it represented. They had not touched paintings, they had not smelled them, they had not been in the presence of them. That makes such an enormous difference. I do think that is why creative people tend to gravitate toward the area where art can be literally experienced.

Q: What interests you about present-day art?

A: One of the most interesting things that's happening in twentieth-century art is the fact that it's made us aware that good and bad art is everywhere. I once saw an exhibition of sewer manhole covers. They were wonderful. They were on the wall of a gallery in New York.

Q: I know you've also selected found objects for display in your loft.

A: What I find interesting about finding an object that is intrinsically beautiful by itself is that outside of its context it can become an art object. In my loft right now is the top of an oil can. It's a round disk with a little bit of writing on that you can't quite read. Two holes in it, one somewhat larger than the other, and diagonally across it a large piece of wood. Somebody might say to me, "This is the top of an oil can, and the board is used to open and close it." Then I can say, "Oh, yes, that's what it is." But if I put it up on a wall, people will come in and say, "Who did that?" It will become an art object, because if you examine it out of its utilitarian context, it can become art. I also have a nineteenth-century mesquite wood wheel from a Mexican cart. To me, it's as beautiful as a Noguchi.

I find this discovery happening frequently. Maybe it is one of the tie-ins I have with utilitarian primitive art. On a high wall in the kitchen, I have a painted board from one of the primitive cultures in the Amazon. It's used as a grinder because it has stones set in it which can be used to grind. It's a beautiful object by itself. It's an art object, a piece of sculpture, though it was never thought of as one. Again, this is the informed taste, an informed eye that can remove things from context. In the Museum of Modern Art and the Metropolitan Museum, there are design sections where they display pots, kettles, and pieces of furniture as art. You can start seeing things outside their context as art objects, and that's very interesting to do.

Q: Outside of their everyday context, do you see these things more as pure form?

A: Yes, but there is a function for these things. These are functional pieces with a form that is their art. They must be comfortable, utilitarian, and beautiful at the same time. The Japanese have done this with their knives, bowls, wooden utensils, and other things.

Q: You have talked about assembling an exhibition of found art objects.

A: I don't know if I would try to mix them. I might find enough found objects and pretend that he was a new artist.

Q: You would call it "art" then.

A: I would call them works by . . . I would make up a name. It would be interesting to see what happened.

Q: It might be a huge success.

A: I wouldn't be surprised—and instructive at the same time.

Q: How do you make a selection among several of one artist's works?

A: My eye works very quickly. I guess I have informed taste, and my instinctive reaction to something always interests me. I see a lot of what passes for great work and may indeed be great works of art, and they don't interest me at all. I don't respond to them intellectually and emotionally at the same time. I may react intellectually *or* emotionally, but unless I get both to something I don't concern myself with it.

Q: When you go to their studios, you seem comfortable talking with artists about their work.

A: I don't give them advice. I always ask many more questions than I do give answers, which if anything makes a direct statement. They seem to find the questions I ask provocative and useful. A few visual artists are close friends.

Q: What does the title of this exhibition mean?

A: Are we going to call it, "Sooner or Later"? The reputations of these artists are just beginning, and I think that, sooner or later, they will be recognized.

Zero Higashida

1991

I WAS WANDERING around Greenwich Village one day a couple of years ago—three, perhaps—minding my own business, by which I mean I had dropped into the New York Studio School to look at a faculty exhibit and had decided to wander about there further, to see what the painting and sculpture students were up to. The stuff was okay—the paintings a little large-gestural figurative for my taste, the sculpture more in a state of idea than realization, perhaps.

Then I turned a corner and came upon some work which stopped me cold, as they say—four or five wooden pieces of various sizes, some assemblage, others disassemblage, all painted dull black. Two thoughts came to mind at once: this is good work!— and, at the same moment—I bet this artist is Japanese! I asked about and got the answer—oh, this guy just uses the space here; he's a Japanese guy.

My instinct having been proved right, I was intrigued. I tracked him down, found he spoke almost no English—and my Japanese, even after four trips to Japan, is limited to survival essentials and superb sushi ordering—but managed to arrange a studio visit, in Brooklyn, nearly under one of the bridges.

There I found—in his tiny space above an auto repair shop—that he worked both huge and small, and in metal as well as in wood. I put three pieces of his in a group exhibit I was curating at the Millwood Gallery on Long Island, and am happy that his worth has been realized by the Philippe Staib Gallery here in New York.

It is not difficult, looking at Zero Higashida's work, to track seeming influences: black painted wood? oh, that's Nevelson; the brutality of gesture? oh, that's Serra. Indeed, a too-quick glance by the instant categorizer at Zero's pieces might lead to such superficial conclusions, but these other artists' ideas are not what Higashida's work is all about. I'm not certain, for that matter, that he knew of either Serra or Nevelson—or a host of other artists—when he fashioned the bed of his aesthetic in Japan.

It is not easy to explain what seems so Japanese about his work to anyone who has not experienced Japan. It all has to do with topography, with landscape, with Zen, with the object as philosophical statement—as unique as isolated, mute, and resonating experience.

Higashida turns the world topsy-turvy as well; gravity in its physical sense is defied, all balances are askew; the gravity of the work itself, its balances are paramount.

Higashida is young; promises are not guarantees; he may eventually abandon isolate work for site experiment—I suspect he will move in that direction. Nothing is sure, but I find this exciting work.

EUGENE IONESCO

1992

WHILE I WASN'T exactly born in a trunk—well I may have been, for I never knew my natural parents, their habits—my adopting family was involved with vaudeville. They were not jugglers or comedians—more's the pity—but owner-management, the Keith Albee Vaudeville Circuit.

The house I tried to grow up in was frequented by performers, and the likes of Ed Wynn and Victor Moore dandled me when I was a tot. My family had me go to the theater when I was a little boy, and my first theatrical memory is of *Jumbo*, at the old Hippodrome—Jimmy Durante and an elephant, great Rodgers and Hart songs, and a toy they hawked in the auditorium to kids like me, a Krazy Kat–like flexible figure on a hand-held board, manipulated from beneath by rings on strings. Doubtless I enjoyed the songs, the elephant, and Durante; I know I loved the toy.

Time passed. I moved through my bewildered adolescence and into my chaotic twenties, accumulating theater experiences on the way. (I was lucky: I lived in New York.)

When I was fourteen—and subject to military school for my sins—I found Shakespeare, and reasoned that the problem was the language; maybe a rewriting, a simplification, would allow us to follow the plots better. I abandoned this theory when I left military school. Later, I experienced Chekhov, Pirandello, Ibsen—feeling no need to rewrite them.

Chance and good fortune took me to the premieres of *The Iceman Cometh* and *The Skin of Our Teeth* and *The Glass Menagerie*. I was still writing not very good poetry then, but had given up on the novel as too much work. I had not yet realized that with the short story—at least in my case—practice does not make perfect, and, in drama, the three-act sex farce I had composed at thirteen had not led me to further attempts at writing plays.

But what an exciting time we all had in New York City in the late forties and fifties—those of us who lived in and with the arts: the concerts of avant-garde music at McMillan Theater at Columbia University, the exhibits of constructivist and abstract expressionist paintings at the galleries, the explosion of foreign authors in translation—Sartre, Camus, the nouvelle vague, the Italian realists Berto, Verga, Moravia, and on and on.

And in the theater in the 1950s there occurred a series of events that changed the rules of playwriting—the premieres in America of plays by that great vaudeville act, Beckett, Ionesco, and Genet.

So profound was the effect of these playwrights that the term "Theater of the Absurd" was invented to encompass (and isolate, alas) their accomplishments. Although Ionesco was the only one of the three for whom the term was valid.

The reactionaries were appalled, the audience for conventional plays was bewildered, and an entire generation of us suddenly decided to be playwrights, liberated by these three. The exuberance, the daring, the sleight-of-hand, the deepest laughter in the deepest dark broke all the rules for us and showed us that the familiar was safe, the predictable was the true Theater of the Absurd.

If we can tie Beckett to the existentialists and Genet to a kind of solitary confinement of the spirit, then we must relate Ionesco to Dadaism and surrealism—movements not a part of mainstream American culture. Ionesco's preoccupation with the collapse of language, as well as such matters as major characters who never appear, furniture (and corpses) growing as the drama proceeds, and people becoming rhinoceroses before our (very) eyes, influenced a lot of us.

As Pinter's debt to Beckett can be found in much of his work, my own stylistic sources for *The American Dream* and *The Sandbox* are clearly to be found in Ionesco. (Indeed, the first several pages of *The American Dream* were so obviously an intended homage to the Romanian-French master that I was startled when some critics insisted it was imitation—an Ionesco-like situation?)

We would diminish Ionesco, however, were we to suggest he was little more than a bag of tricks. His concerns with individual freedom, identity, and rationalism place him higher than that. He was a major force in shaping nontraditional drama in the second half of the twentieth century.

Beckett has gone on to be an acknowledged master, albeit almost buried by the scholars; Genet is still sniffed suspiciously by the wary, who are profoundly frightened by the primal violence of his vision, and Ionesco—the most playful of the three, the most purely "experimental," though every bit as reality grounded and tough as the others—has been neglected.

There's no point in dwelling on this. A hundred years down the line—unless the viruses have taken over—we'll see it all sort itself out.

And now Ionesco can write no longer; he has joined the others. As a character I like says, in a play I admire, "That particular vaudeville act is playing the cloud circuit now."

What an act it was, and what a hard act to follow!

ALAN SCHNEIDER

1992

I AM A bit like Tennessee Williams's Blanche, who tells what ought to be true rather than necessarily what is. I have a mind somewhat like a sieve. I can remember very little that I read, very little that I experience—remember it consciously—but I have noticed that when I'm writing a play, a character in the play can remember and quote from a poem that I cannot recall having read.

I also have a healthy disregard for sources. Listening to things that Alan had said, I think, "Isn't it interesting that Alan agreed with me so much?" In the back of my mind I had the creeping awareness that indeed much of what I think and much of what I say is the result of those things that Alan taught me. But we do reverse as time goes on in the same way that many art critics and drama critics today, reviewing a work written, oh, eight years ago, insist on how much it influenced a work written twenty years before it.

Alan taught me a great deal about playwriting, and he taught me a good deal about direction. No, that's not true. Alan did not teach me anything about playwriting. Alan taught me a good deal of what it is like to *be* a playwright. You cannot teach anybody anything about playwriting, in the same you way cannot teach anybody to *be* a playwright. I teach at the University of Houston, and I think of myself as refereeing events in the theater. You cannot teach a person who is not a playwright how to write a play like himself. You can teach a person who is not a playwright how to write a play like somebody else, and, in the usual "monkey see, monkey do" fashion, you can probably end up with a terrible imitation of what the other playwright has done. Nor can you teach a playwright—a natural born playwright—how to write a play. You can merely point him in the direction of the least pernicious influences, and perhaps reveal to him his own nature as a playwright. I'm convinced that we have in this country right now (I'll make up a number) five or six very good playwrights who have never written a play. It has never been revealed to them that they are playwrights. They *are* playwrights because being a playwright is *who* you are and less what you do. So, no, Alan did not teach me about playwriting. He taught me about being a playwright. He made me conscious of what I was doing, of what I had been doing, and he made me think the way a playwright should think.

When Alan and I began working on *The American Dream* and on to *Virginia Woolf* and other projects, I had not learned that I was expected to know what I had done. I had assumed that having done it was sufficient. But Alan would come to discussions—and Alan and I met many times before rehearsals of a play began, for hours on end—and Alan would come with a thick notebook; he soon enough revealed that this notebook was filled with questions about what I had done. I was expected to be able to answer every single question that he asked me about not only the intention of the play, the intention of the particular situation in the play, but the characters themselves, their nature, their background. Alan would ask me questions that at first surprised me but then ultimately merely revealed that he was trying to get out of me that which I *had,* but had never before articulated. He made me aware that I *did know* the subtext and the history of all the characters that I had written, but I hadn't thought about it.

Alan was aware, as a profoundly good director should be, that the only thing that you can direct is the only thing that an actor can act: the nature of the character and the moment-to-moment truth and the reality of what is happening to the character in that particular situation.

Alan did enormous homework—ran me dry, made me aware, made me think about things to such an extent that I remember occasionally, when I no longer had any answers, could no longer recall what I had intended by a certain thing that Alan would keep on pressing, that I would make things up. Fortunately, most of the things that I made up were true, and so we didn't have any serious problem.

There is nothing—well, there are two or three things, but there is close to nothing—worse for a playwright than to come to the first day of rehearsal and discover that the director of his play is planning to direct a play considerably different from that which he thought he wrote. You would be surprised, perhaps, how frequently this occurs. You would also, perhaps, not be so surprised to know there are a number of directors who come into rehearsal thinking they know a good deal more about the play than the playwright does, and that the playwright's vision of his play should be properly secondary to the director's vision of himself as director. Alan was not one of these people. Alan did understand that he was there to serve the play. He understood, aside from occasional commercial needs, that there is really no point in going into rehearsal (A) with a play that you don't respect, and (B) that is not really ready to open. Why go into rehearsal with a play that needs a great deal of work?

I have been content to rely on my instinct as a playwright and to assume that everything that I put down was justified and had a proper basis. Alan's opening me up has not done any damage to me as a playwright, I think. The act of creation, the act of writing a play, remains to me as much a mystery as it was at the very beginning. My reliance on the creative act, which resides some-where deep in the unconscious, is as complete as it ever was. But Alan persuaded me that once I had relied upon the unconscious, it was my responsibility to translate that coherently into con-sciousness. This probably has helped me as a playwright. It cer-tainly has helped me, along with Alan's instructions, in being a director.

What I have learned as a director has a good deal to do with what I learned from Alan. God knows, if you are a director, you damn well better know the text. You'd better know the script. If the author is around, find out from the author. If the author is not around, do some research and make some enormously intelligent guesses. Find out what, indeed, the author had intended. Be one step ahead of everybody. Do not ever find yourself in the place where anybody can ask you a question which you don't have an answer for. It doesn't have to be the right answer, because you can always correct it later. But don't ever find yourself in the posi-tion that you don't have an answer. Comprehend that most problems in the production of a play with actors have nothing to do with the text, but have everything to do with the subtext, have everything to do with incorrect subtextual choices that the actor has possibly made. I learned something infinitely more important—and this applied to me especially since I was both author and director of a number of the plays that I was working on—that there is no such thing as an absolute subtext. There is only the truth. There is only the subtext. The truth is in what happens. Every actor will use a slightly different way of getting to that particular truth. There is no absolute truth in subtext. There is only absolute truth in text.

The briefest of examples of this. I directed *The Zoo Story* twelve or fifteen times over the years. In one production, the actor playing Jerry (it was Ben Piazza, who was splendid in that play, and was, and still is, a good, actor) came up to me because he was playing Jerry. And he said, "Edward, when Jerry was growing up, did he have a dog?" A dog is very important in *The Zoo Story*, the landlady's dog. And I thought for a moment, and I tried to remember what I as author had thought, but then I realized, "No, no, don't do that. Do not impose the author on the director. You are the director of this play. Talk to the author. Go talk to him some other time. Talk to your actor as the director." And I thought about Ben for a little bit, and what Ben could use best, and I said, "Yes, yes, when you were a kid, you and your family lived"—I made all this up—"you and your family lived on a chicken farm in New Jersey about forty-seven miles outside of New York City, and there were lots of animals around. Your father had mostly chickens. But there were horses and some goats and sheep and there were six dogs." I named the dogs for him; I told him what kind of dogs they were. Ben nodded; we never discussed the matter again; it ended up being a very good production of the play.

Twelve years after that: another production of *The Zoo Story* with different actors, same author, same director, however. Damned if the actor playing Jerry didn't ask me the same question. But he didn't say, "Did Jerry have a dog when he was growing up?" He said, "When I was growing up, did I have a dog?" Now, I knew he wasn't playing Twenty Questions with me. He did not mean, did he as the actor have a dog when he was growing up. He meant, when Jerry was growing up did Jerry have a dog? I remembered, of course, since you don't have these occurrences all the time, I remembered what I told Ben Piazza. But then I stopped myself. I said, "Uh-uh. That's not going to work with this actor." I decided that this actor could work much better with deprivation, and so I said to him, "No, no, you had no pets when you were growing up. You loved animals, but your father hated animals, and he wouldn't let you have a pet, a dog. When you were six years old"—my author's creativity working here beautifully—"when you were six years old," I said, "you brought a little puppy home and your father drowned it."

Which is true? Both. Obviously. The truth in that instance is what the actor can use to become the character. I must have learned this, as I learned so much else, from Alan: that the subtext *modulates* and varies according to the needs of the actor; that the character is sacrosanct—the actor must become the character. When I direct a play I don't really care how an actor gets to my destination, as long as he gets to my destination. Alan was not particularly concerned with whatever methods he had to use to get to the author's destination, as long as he got to the author's destination.

Last night I was reading from Nabokov's *Strong Opinions,* a group of essays and letters and responses to critics. Nabokov was replying to a review by a critic, who had found sexual symbolism in just about every line that Nabokov wrote, especially *Lolita*. Whenever Nabokov would make mention of a pen or a pencil, quite clearly Nabokov was referring to a penis. Even Nabokov's little puns were all highly phallic; the critic suggested that in one of Nabokov's books the fact that in a soccer game somebody was kicking the ball through into the goal box, was obviously a reference to an attempt to enter the vagina. Nabokov interjected at that point: an orifice which the critic for some bizarre reason thinks of as square.

I have evolved a theory on all this nonsense, which is simply this: if anybody comes up with some ideas as to the content, interpretation, meaning of a play of mine which diminishes what I know I intended, the critic is wrong. If, however, the critic comes up with content, ideas, etc. that make me an infinitely more interesting, complex, and intelligent playwright than I know myself to be, then of course that is correct. This is not necessarily a fallacy, because unless a critic goes a very long way out his way in order to be wrong (and it is amazing to me the number who can and will), it is very difficult for him to find things in a work of art that are not already there. We work through the unconscious. We do a great number of things as creative people that we are not consciously aware that we have done. We have things revealed to us from time to time. Oh, I didn't know I had done that. Well, obviously I did. So, we should take credit for them.

We know, we writers, I think we know what we intended, and I think we are not surprised if somebody comes up and informs us of that which we intended without being consciously aware of it. I think, equally well, we know when some know-nothing comes up with something that is totally wrong. And while we cannot necessarily prove it, we know. And if they would come to us more frequently, they would be in less trouble, but, of course, they would publish a good deal less.

JONATHAN THOMAS

1993

ART CAN BE about anything, and it can employ whatever means it wishes to succeed to that intention; art must be judged by how well it succeeds to its intention and whether that intention is worth the trouble of succeeding to. Lesser art does little to disturb the status quo; it is, of course, equally true that art which disturbs, provokes, renunciates, or tries to do serious damage to established artistic coherence does not necessarily succeed in moving out of the "lesser" status simply by its agressiveness.

What must happen for art to become a major factor in our aesthetic perceptions is that it must expand (relocate?) our judgmental boundries and, at the same time, be a "moral" act, in that it allows the logics and coherencies of art to affect—and effect—our responses to the world around us and its quandries.

To the extent that we permit the arts to impinge upon our consciousness we are altered; our perceptions are either honed or dulled and our moral comprehensions are either broadened or diminished. Art can enliven, and art can kill.

It shocks me every time I write of these matters that I need do so, but as I see the chasm between what is desired and what is to *be* desired in the arts deepening, the mind-deadening excesses of our popular entertainments, and the lemming-like drive by our majority critics toward middlebrowism, I see that the battle is never unjoined, that there need be—perhaps at best—a holding action against the corruptions of our arts values.

The concept that "high art" need be a minority participation in a democrary stems, we must assume, from the appalling lack of arts education in this country; otherwise, we must assume that we are populated by philistines and the retarded. We know that this latter is not so, and we keep hoping that what *can* be *will* be.

Institutions like the Wadsworth Atheneum, through its Matrix program, can help tilt the balance in the direction of sustained and useful dialogue between those who make art and those for whom they take the trouble, if you will. The Matrix program has been going on for a long time now, and has exposed the public to a host of provocative, innovative, disturbing, and thoroughly fine artists. It has served the noble double function of presenting the artists to a larger public and broadening the public's awareness of the possibilities of art.

Which brings us to Jonathan Thomas—an artist who fulfills the criteria mentioned earlier, who combines audacity, intelligence and talent in equal parts. Even a quick look at his work will make it evident that more is going on than meets the eye and mind at first glance. Exactly what *are* these paintings about, these elegant, brooding, somber abstractions which suddenly become—in revealing their materials—disturbing messages, private and yet communicative, and which then go on to rebecome what we first apprehended, though deepened?

It is this vibration—this cross-fade—between the explicit and the implicit, between the totality and its construction, which gives these paintings their disturbing magic.

The varying sizes of the paintings determine the order of response. The huge *Big Black Upright* (1992) will not reveal its methods until after its sum has accosted one; *American Descent* (1991) must go through three stages of approach: before its particulars come into focus one must penetrate first either its symbolisms or its overall presence; while *Study Number Twelve* (1992) or its equally small brother paintings, seem to want to be viewed in the reverse—elements first, totality after.

Thomas did not come to painting as a profession as young as some do. While it is true that he painted and drew as an adolescent—portraits of dogs and of other family members— his university studies in pure mathematics and art history led him to a period of absorption and consideration; dance and architecture occupied him—as forms as much as art—and it was not until several years after he finished his formal training that he realized painting—as practice, though not as a limiting definition (he has made sculpture)—should be his life's work.

I have watched the development of his art carefully now for over fifteen years—in his studio, and in his continuing museum and gallery exposures—and I am convinced that he has come strongly into his own, has matured into a complexity of substance and effect both intellectually challenging and aesthetically satisfying.

To my mind, the flow of dance, the solidity of architecture, the logic of mathematics, and the accesses of art history have combined in his work to allow the creation of highly individual art.

His early work—an examination of the conclusions of the

Constructivists—was, inevitably, I suspect, provoked by Thomas's university focus on pure mathematics. He moved then to explore the implications and resonances of the stuttering cubism of Balla and Severini, and—most important—Marcel Duchamp's *Nude Descending a Staircase*. The process then was to what I would fine as a kind of intellectually controlled abstract expressionism.

Thomas has always been deeply interested in what art does *to* us, not merely what it does *for* us. And in his new work he has jumped full mind and talent into an examination of the conditioning of our responses by the media, of the mind-deadening effect of commercial advertising—how the repetition of image and idea has become the reality determinant of our era.

This is merely a starting place for Thomas, however. He is not content with art as social commentary, or even philosophical examination; he is determined to make art which functions as art on its own terms, and it is this double strategy which enables his work to escape the art traps referred to earlier.

Starting with such commonplace objects as men's underwear, jeans, etc.—everywhere with us: billboards, TV—he has transmuted these almost entirely out of context (see Picasso's sculpture of the bull's head made from bicycle parts, for example), using them as a painting surface. They move back and forth intellectually between what they were and what they have become. While so many contemporary artists are imitating the recent artistic past, turning it into a kind of commerce, Thomas is beginning with commercial excess and redefining it as art.

Geometric elements are imposed on the painting surface; entire areas are indented or incised (see *Figures Descending*, 1901); the painting surfaces often resemble metal (see *Monochromes, Falling,* 1991). Glue, wood, cloth, and paint meld to produce an organic whole greater than the sum of the parts. In a way, these paintings resemble sculpture—relief, certainly. They cannot be "entered" as most painting can; the interplay of falling and supporting elements is intentionally two-dimensional.

The resulting experience is art which is not "poetic" in a limiting sense, but is confrontational, ironic, and complex. Thomas's work must be experienced comprehensively for its full effect: a mere glance does it little justice. What is essential is the intense presence of the viewer in the intense presence of the art.

Some Thoughts on Sculpture

1993

I HAVEN'T LOOKED up the dictionary definition of sculpture lately, but I'm sure that even in the most recent editions of these books the description contains phrases and words such as three-dimensional art, objects, carved or modeled, plastic, constructed, tactile, spatial, built-up, reduced, etc., etc., but no catalogue will be complete, will do the trick. For sculpture mutates faster than any other art form I know of.

I have—for example—seen a sculpture made out of laser light—parallel, abutting, intersecting, and independent shafts of it—quite beautiful, haunting, even; but that was not the half of it: each patterning of laser light lasted but for a brief period; then some element (or elements) of it changed, creating a wholly different and new light sculpture, and since the duration of each individual shaft as well as the change of the totality was programmed randomly, there emerged an endlessly varied series of sculptures.

As well, I have seen a sculpture created out of the spaces between or within objects—wholly negative space. (Not a shoebox shape, say, as the sculptural object, but entire empty space *within* as the sculpture.)

So, defining sculpture—limiting it—has become difficult. There are paintings far thicker than certain flat wall sculptures; there are multicolored three-dimensional objects which say "painting!" loudly, and do not suggest to me that they are anything else. Appropriation and context confuse the issue even more. I recall going into a gallery many years ago and coming upon an exhibit of round wall pieces, metal and maybe two inches thick. Each of them was of a slightly different diameter, but they all had one thing in common—an indented and raised patterning. They were mysterious and ugly-beautiful as they hung and breathed there, bathed in the gallery lighting. I was impressed and was about to seek out the name of the artist (for it was evidently all the work of one mind) when I suddenly realized what I was looking at—a series of manhole covers, transformed by new context into art . . . which raises the question, "Were they always art in spite of intention?"

It was a defining moment for me in the comprehension of the illimits of art—as much as anything by Duchamp, or the Dadaists, and far more than, say, the toy automobile or the bicycle handlebars Picasso manipulated, for in them was a wit (or joke) which said, "Look at me! look at me!" Nor can I walk down a street in New York City now and come upon one of those giant metal rectangles they use to plug up street holes—I think that's what they do with them—the plates quite smooth except for the scarring of a letter or numeral or two, and sometimes a corner hole for lifting—without stopping and admiring what, to my eye, is as much art as a lot (most!) of what I see passing in the commercial galleries and museums.

What the hell *is* art then—what we define it as? Must it be intentional as art? If that is so then hundreds of years of amazing African carving was not art when it was made—utilitarian as it was—until our aesthetic and our commerce defined it so.

And I suppose I must raise here the unnerving thought of what exactly is (would be) an exhibit of wall sculptures constructed to resemble manhole covers, which would—by a double magic— transform themselves back into art.

Enough of that.

In this exhibit are pieces I have accumulated—along with many others—over the years of "looking around." I would guess the average age of the artists represented in this exhibit to be around thirty-five. Few of the artists are household names, and while John Duff, Mia Westerlund Roosen, and Ellen Phelan are getting there, the works here were done long before that process began. Five of the artists are women, and all but four are from the United States. (Anne Thulin is Swedish and Alistair Milne is Scotts, though these days you will find him in New York; Wendy Smith is British, and Jonathan Thomas is Canadian by birth.)

I suppose the unifying force behind all the work—though individuality here is paramount—is tripart: deep involvement with materials and the artist's hand in using them; abstraction, in that they all are more concerned with ideas about sculpture as an idea than representation; and adventure—the willingness to go way out on a limb.

Some of the pieces exhibited here are quite "ugly," for which read "beautiful." Some are quirky. Some may seem hermetic (until you breathe with them for a while.) And they all are dangerous, in that they do not leave our perceptions unaltered. They are about the redefinition of sculpture, and *that*—aside from their individual qualities—is why they are gathered here.

Enjoy.

ON *THREE TALL WOMEN*

1994

PEOPLE OFTEN ASK me how long it takes me to write a play, and I tell them "all of my life." I know that's not the answer they're after—what they really want is some sense of the time between the first glimmer of the play in my mind and the writing down, and perhaps the duration of the writing down—but "all of my life" is the truest answer I can give, for it is the only one which is exact, since the thinking about the play and the putting it to paper vary so from play to play.

Few sensible authors are happy discussing the creative process—it is, after all, black magic, and may lose its power if we look that particular gift horse too closely in the mouth, or anywhere else, for that matter; further, since the creative process cannot be taught or learned, but only described, of what use is the discussion? Still, along with "where do your ideas come from?" the question is greatly on the mind of that tiny group of civilians who bother to worry it at all.

With *Three Tall Women* I can pinpoint the instant I began

writing it, for it coincides with my first awareness of consciousness. I was in a group of four who were on a knoll (I could even
now show you the exact spot, the exact knoll) observing the completion of a new house, the scaffolding still on it. There were three
adults and tiny me—my adoptive mother, my adoptive father, my
nanny (Nanny Church) and, in Nanny Church's arms—what?
three-month-old Edward, certainly no older. My memory of the
incident is wholly visual—the scaffolding, the people; and while I
have no deep affection for it, it *is* my first awareness of being
aware, and so I suppose I treasure it.

I have the kind of mind that does not retain much consciously—
I experience, absorb, consider, banish into the deeps. Oh, should
someone remind me of a significant event, its sights and sounds
will come flooding back, but free of emotional baggage—that dealt
with at the time of the incident, or catalogued elsewhere. And I
know that my present self is shaped by as much self-deception as
anyone else's, that my objectivities are guided by the maps I myself
have drawn, and that nothing is really ever forgotten, merely filed
away as inconvenient or insupportable.

So, when I decided to write what became *Three Tall Women,* I
was more aware of what I did *not* want to do than exactly what
I did want to accomplish. I knew my subject—my adoptive
mother, whom I knew from my infancy (that knoll!) until her
death over sixty years later, and who, perhaps, knew me as well.
Perhaps.

I knew I did not want to write a revenge piece—could not hon-
estly do so, for I felt no need for revenge. We had managed to
make each other very unhappy over the years, but I was past all
that, though I think she was not. I harbor no ill will toward her;
it is true I did not like her much, could not abide her prejudices,

her loathings, her paranoias, but I did admire her pride, her sense of self. As she moved toward ninety, began rapidly failing both physically and mentally, I was touched by the survivor, the figure clinging to the wreckage only partly of her own making, refusing to go under.

No, it was not a revenge piece I was after, and I was not interested in "coming to terms" with my feelings toward her. I knew my feelings, I thought they were pretty much on the mark, and knew that I would not move much beyond the grudging respect I'd slowly developed for her. I was not seeking self-catharsis, in other words.

I realized then that what I wanted to do was write as objective a play as I could about a fictional character who resembled in every way, in every event, someone I had known very, very well. And it was only when I invented, when I translated fact intact into fiction, that I was aware I would be able to be accurate without prejudice, objective without the distortive folly of "interpretation."

I did not cry and gnash my teeth as I put this woman down on paper. I cannot recall suffering either *with* her or because of her as I wrote her. I recall being very interested in what I was doing—fascinated by the horror and sadness I was (re)creating.

Writers have the schizophrenic ability to both participate in their lives and, at the same time, observe themselves participating in their lives. Well . . . some of us have this ability, and I suspect it was this (frightening?) talent that allowed me to write *Three Tall Women* without prejudice, if you will.

I know that I "got her out of my system" by writing this play, but then again I get *all* the characters in *all* of my plays out of my system by writing about them.

Finally, when I based the character "Grandma" (*The American Dream, The Sandbox*) on my own (adoptive) maternal grandmother, I noticed that while I liked the lady a lot—we were in alliance against those folk in the middle—the character I created was both funnier and more interesting than the model. Have I done that here? Is the woman I wrote in *Three Tall Women* more human, more multifaceted than its source? Very few people who met my adoptive mother in the last twenty years of her life could abide her, while many people who have seen my play find her fascinating. Heavens, what have I done?!

THIRTY-FIVE YEARS ON

1996

IT'S ODD, ISN'T it, that so many contemporary playwrights are best known for one play, usually an early one and, while often a very good one, not necessarily their finest work. Say Osborne and most people would come up with *Look Back in Anger;* say Pinter and the response so often is *The Birthday Party;* Stoppard: *Rosencrantz and Guildenstern Are Dead.* Say Beckett and, more often than not you get *Waiting for Godot;* Ionesco and *The Bald Soprano;* Genet: *The Maids.* In the United States say Arthur Miller and nine out of ten would reply *Death of a Salesman,* Tennessee Williams and *A Streetcar Named Desire.* (Eugene O'Neill is the exception here: the late play *Long Day's Journey into Night* is the mind-jerk response.)

And I find *Who's Afraid of Virginia Woolf?* hung about my neck like a shining medal of some sort—very nice but a trifle onerous.

Living playwrights bristle a little at this sort of shorthand, for we all insist—hope?—that we haven't written our best works yet, and we all harbor deep, almost religious faith in our most dismissed or despised efforts.

All of the plays I mentioned above are fine works—and the playwrights are fine writers—but each of them has written one or two (or more!) plays which I consider the equal (at least!) of the "signature" ones. But . . . it's nice to be known for something, and we all take it where we can get it, and it's nice to be admired for something we're proud of.

Who's Afraid of Virginia Woolf? was my fifth play (the fifth I'll admit to—there was some juvenilia) following on four hour-long-or-less full-length if not full-evening ones. Its length—nearly three hours of playing time—almost equaled that of the four previous ones together, and it was the first of my plays (in America) to be performed in a large commercial arena.

The facts are—no pride here; pleasure, yes—that it was a huge commercial and critical success, and changed me from a known commodity into a household name. Fine. Very nice, if a little troubling. It was as if, suddenly, the gifted little boy (*The Zoo Story,* etc.) had, by magic, become a grown-up, while, to my mind, the fifteen-minute *The Sandbox* had succeeded as well to an equally valid artistic intention. But . . . off-Broadway is not Broadway, and fifteen minutes is not three hours, and experimentation is not the same as (seeming) naturalism.

Please don't misunderstand me: I'm very happy to have written *Who's Afraid of Virginia Woolf?* I think it's a fine play, and its continued success over the past thirty-five years has contributed to the freedom I feel to pursue my career as I have seen fit, and if there *is* a history years from now, and if I am a footnote in it, I daresay *Who's Afraid of Virginia Woolf?* will be the play identi-fied with my name (or my name with it), and I, in my shallow grave, will not cavil much.

A DELICATE BALANCE

A NONRECONSIDERATION

1996

MY MIND IS going, I suspect; I have no idea how long I've known most of my friends; the names of most people are beyond me, and I cannot recall the emotional or physical experience of the writing of most of my plays, or how long ago the experience I cannot recall occurred.

The only senses I fully retain—and very sharply these—are picture images and sounds. Hearing two bars of almost any piece of serious music has me naming the composer, the piece, and often the date of composition and opus number—or K., or Hoboken, or whatever. Seeing a painting for a second time—in a new context, of course—has me instantly recalling on what wall it hung, in what room, in what country, when I saw it first.

But names and events . . . that's another matter. Once I looked straight at my mother and couldn't figure out who she was. (Well, I guess we've all had that one!)

So . . . is it *really* thirty years since the first production of *A Delicate Balance*? It seems like yesterday, as they say? No, certainly not . . . but thirty years?

The play has not changed; that *I* can see. I've had to rewrite only two lines—making it clear that topless bathing suits (for women, of course) are not made anymore, and changing "our dear Republicans as dull as ever" to "as brutal as ever" (that second change long overdue).

The play does not seem to have "dated"; rather, its points seem clearer now to more people than they were in its lovely first production. Now, in its lovely new production (I will not say "revival"; the thing was not dead—unseen, unheard perhaps, but lurking), it seems to me exactly the same experience. No time has passed; the characters have not aged or become strange. (The upper-upper-middle-class WASP culture has *always* been just a little bizarre, of course.)

The play concerns—as it always has, in spite of early-on critical misunderstanding—the rigidity and ultimate paralysis which afflicts those who settle in too easily, waking up one day to discover that all the choices they have avoided no longer give them any freedom of choice, and that what choices they do have left are beside the point.

I have become odder with time, I suppose (my next play but one will be about a goat, for God's sake), but *A Delicate Balance,* bless it, does not seem to have changed much—aged nicely, perhaps. Could we all say the same.

Interview with Steve Capra

1996

SC: You've expressed impatience with critics who—you use the term "hunt the symbol." How can a critic help us to discuss drama without inappropriately *stressing* things? What contributions should critics be making?

EA: Well, the first question that comes up is "What is the basic function of criticism?" Are you talking about reviewing, or are you talking about scholarly criticism here? Let's take an analogy of classical music rather than drama for a moment. I wanted to be a composer when I was a kid, having studied Bach and Mozart and all those types, but I didn't make it because I was incompetent, and it wasn't what I was supposed to be doing. I know a great deal about classical music. I have on my shelves lots of books on composers and their music—a very, very good book on Beethoven's string quartets, which analyzes each one, goes through it page by page.

   And I know the Beethoven string quartets backwards and forwards, both, very well. I know their intellectual and emotional content. Those books are of very minor importance to me. I don't need them. I'm not convinced the equivalent scholarly work on a play is of any more value than that. A play is a piece of literature to begin with, which has the added virtue of being able to be performed, and so people can experience it one of two ways. Either on the page, read, as a literary experience, or the other way, as a performed piece. The folly is to think that a play exists completely only in performance. That's absurd. A Beethoven string quartet—to somebody who knows how to read music—can be heard by reading it. A play can be heard and seen by reading it. But most people don't know how to read music, and most people don't bother to read plays—or even know how to read a play intelligibly—so it would seem.

The scholarly work that is done is of interest to other scholars, I think. Not to anybody else. The black magic that makes any work of art any good escapes the careful analysis of any scholar. An engine of a car works—you can find exactly how it works—*exactly* how it works—every mechanical thing that makes the whole thing work. That has nothing to do with why an automobile engine exists. An automobile engine exists because somebody saw the need for the automobile engine to exist, and found a way to make that necessity occur. Same thing with a piece of literature, with a play. How the person puts it together—how the playwright puts it together—all the structure, and the rest of it—is minor compared to the need and the urgency in that which created the piece in the first place.

But, of course, most critics are not scholars. Most critics are there, unfortunately, to make the theater safe for the audience, rather than the dangerous experience it should be. Also, everybody should always keep in mind that no critic is ever maintained on the staff of any magazine or newspaper unless the owner or the publisher wants him to be there. No critic is kept unless he or she reflects the taste and needs of the organ for which this critic works. You have to keep *that* in mind. So what used to be my attack on critics—I've come to realize—really shouldn't be. They are hired hands, for the most part. And they will not keep their jobs unless, consciously or unconsciously, they cotton to the attitude that the owners want them to.

SC: But certainly the theater needs all the help it can get . . .

EA: It needs all the help it can get, yes, but it certainly doesn't need the supposed help of a bunch of critics who are trying to make it safe, who are trying to do—as Walter Kerr once said, in a radio interview years ago—quote—"I consider it my function as a drama critic to reflect what I consider to be the tastes of the readers of the newspaper for which I work"—unquote. The critic who's there, supposedly creating taste, considering it his responsibility to reflect the existing taste. Of course theater needs all the help it can possibly get, but a lot of the supposed help it receives is killing it—just really killing it.

I have never seen a straight play on the Broadway theater in New York that has ever gotten the money reviews that a musical has gotten—ever. This is simply because the musicals are what everybody seems to want to be popular. They bring in more advertising dollars to the newspapers. They bring in much more money to the Broadway community—restaurants and hotels and all the rest of them. So there's so many unfairnesses and so many things going on—this particular help doesn't help much. Serious drama just doesn't do well in the commercial theater anymore. Unfortunately, the audiences at commercial theater are for the most part upper-middle-class, wealthy whites—which really has nothing to do with what theater should be all about in this country.

SC: You've also said that you write so intuitively that you don't always understand intellectually every point of your work.

EA: That's a slight misstatement of what I said. There is the conscious mind and the unconscious mind. The play moves from the unconscious to the conscious mind. By the time a play has moved completely to the conscious mind and I put it down on paper, I'm pretty much aware of what metaphors and symbols people will find in the piece. There are occasionally some things that I learn, but I've never learned anything accurate about a play of mine that I wasn't able to say when I learned it, "Well, of course, that's what I intended." I never learned anything contradictory to what I, in my gut, knew was my intention.

SC: Do critics at least help to articulate these points so that most people can recognize them?

EA: I don't understand why people have to go to a play with a scorecard. I think they should be told, "This is a fucking good play which advances the theater, and it's going to be a disturbing and marvelous experience for you. Go see it!" I don't think the thing should be analyzed. I don't think the plot should be told. Nobody reviewing a new piece of music gives us the tunes. They don't do that.

SC: But most people think so much drama is inaccessible.

EA: It's not inaccessible. It's totally accessible! Sometimes it's a little different in form from what people expect. If *Waiting for Godot* had been set in a living room, nobody would have had any trouble with it. It's this fucking blasted *heath* that got in everybody's way. They see a strange setting—they see something that is not naturalistic—automatically the warning flags go up. They say, "I'm not going to be able to understand this." And therefore, they can't understand it, because they're determined they're not going to. There's nothing in any Beckett play that I've ever experienced that is inaccessible to anybody with a reasonable mind.

SC: Certain plays of yours have been more successful, critically, and in terms of popularity, than others. Can we generalize . . .

EA: The most naturalistic ones have been—yes—of course, because American theater—as opposed to European theater—is based on naturalism. We don't like the political, intellectual theater of Brecht; we don't like the stylized theater of the European avant-garde much. We like good, old-fashioned, naturalistic plays. Any play that wanders far from those boundaries is in trouble. And the plays of mine that have been most successful have all been naturalistic ones. *The Zoo Story,* for what it's worth, is a naturalistic play—so's *Who's Afraid of Virginia Woolf?*—so's *A Delicate Balance.*

SC: *Seascape* . . .

EA: So's *Seascape*—sure—that's a naturalistic play.

SC: Do European audiences—in Vienna, London . . .

EA: They respond more equally to the stylized as well as naturalistic plays—yes. Well, some of the influence of the American theater is beginning to hit London now—the West End is not quite as adventuresome as it should be. Thank heavens for the fringe theaters and the RSC, and the Almeida, and the National, and the Royal Court. Without those, the West End would look just like Broadway, unfortunately.

SC: Some time ago, you said: "I get criticized for not having the catharsis in the body of the play. I don't think that's where the catharsis should be. I think it should take place in the mind of the spectator sometimes afterwards—maybe a year after experiencing the play."

EA: I think that's one of the interesting things that happened with twentieth-century drama—that it moved the catharsis out of the body of the play.

SC: But up to a year after seeing the play?

EA: Well, it depends. Sometimes you get things quick—sometimes you don't. You can't comprehend anything unless you can relate it somehow to the limitations and parameters of your own experience. I just don't think everything should be tied up in a nice bundle so you don't have to worry about it after you leave the theater.

SC: In light of the fact that there are film and television, can theater regain the popularity it had for Ibsen's audience, or its importance as a disseminator of ideas?

EA: Well, for a time in this country, before there was television and there really was serious film, there was a short period there where people saw American plays—up to about 1910. Then film started coming in and people started going to film, and then television, sound film, and all the rest of it. No, I don't think it ever will have the popularity it did, for a whole variety of reasons—price, for one. Television—my God! You just sit there and it comes to you! Plays don't come to you—you have to go to them. Movies are preposterously expensive—I think seven-fifty or eight dollars a ticket to see something that is not a real experience, but a photograph of a past experience, and a fantasy experience.

SC: And very naturalistic.

EA: Plays of course are ridiculously expensive, but even when they're not ridiculously expensive, people don't want to go see them because they are real experience. They're not safe fantasy experience. There's something about the reality of a play experience that's disturbing to a lot of people. You go to a movie, and you sit there with your popcorn and your Coke, and you watch people shooting people's heads off, and brains splashing against walls and things like that. It has no effect on you whatever. You try any kind of physical violence onstage, if you duplicate something like that, people would run vomiting out of the theater, because it's a real experience. It is happening at the time. The reality of the theater experience is the one thing that makes it—for me—far more exciting than most filmed experiences ever could be—because it is happening at the moment. And our suspension of disbelief is a totally different kind.

SC: I understand you're saying that the American public is very hooked on naturalism. It's always difficult to educate an audience to a new form. Is there something about naturalism that is more seductive than . . .

EA: Well, it doesn't demand that we use our imaginations. "Oh, that, yes—my family, my friends live there—in that living room, in that kitchen. Yes, that's the way my friends talk. Yes, of course."

SC: So drama has reached a point—or chanced upon a form—
that it would be more difficult to move away from than . . .

EA: Well, we always had naturalistic plays in the United States.
Some of them were more fantastic than others, I thought—
but you look at American drama around the turn of the century. With the possible exception of *The Scarecrow*, Percy
McKaye's play, most of them are really quite naturalistic.
Some of them fairly melodramatic, but, I mean, the first people
who made serious experiments in America were Sophie Tread-
well and Elmer Rice—the late twenties. There were some
experiments that were made—*The Machinal* is a good experimental play. Elmer Rice's *The Adding Machine,* around
1930—an experimental play. We don't have very many.

SC: If a play changes the spectator unconsciously, you've also
said that it will be translated into social action—political
action.

EA: Indirectly, sometimes. Because how we vote, how we
respond to the world around us, socially and politically, is
determined by our concept of ourselves. And our concept of
ourselves *can* be formulated by the arts. And should be. And
so if a play can make us realize that we're skimming along,
we're really not grabbing—participating—in our own lives,
and we're letting other people do all the stuff we should
do—if that nagging thought can be put in us, then maybe
we'll change a little bit. Maybe we'll start being more
socially and politically responsible animals.

SC: But can we translate into political terms what that means?

EA: Well, aside from some agitprop plays which are very highly
specifically political, agitprop plays have turned out not to
be terribly good, as opposed to, in Germany, Brecht and

other people. Their agitprop plays were better than agit-prop. They were deeply political, socially involved plays. In this country most agitprop plays weren't terribly good. . . . But, if a play can make us more aware of our failings, our responsibilities, to ourselves and others, then it may be able to change us into better people. Movies won't do this, gen-erally. Because movies are a fantasy experience and we know we're not supposed to pay any attention.

SC: But people do pay attention, at least in terms of going to them. They're so much more accessible.

EA: Going to them, but I don't know that they necessarily learn much. Maybe the people who went to see *Burnt by the Sun*. Did you see it? Maybe the people who went to see *Burnt by the Sun* learned something. Maybe they did. But not many people went to see it. It's the Russian film about Stalin's execution of the final Bolsheviks in the middle thir-ties. Glorious film. One of the finest films of the past ten or fifteen years.

SC: I'll remember it. I think you addressed an Outwrite Confer-ence several years ago, and you criticized gay writers for becoming ghettoized, is that right?

EA: Yes. My point was that everybody belongs to many minorities—many. I pointed out that I belong to a number of minorities. There are more women than men in the world, the minority being the male. I'm a minority by having white skin; I'm a minority by being educated—even a smaller minority by being a creative writer—and all sorts of minorities, and down there at the end, I happen to be gay—another minority. My identity is created by all of them, not by any one of them, and my objection was to those gay writers who felt that their identity was created by the fact that they were gay. Therefore I made a distinction between gay writers and writers who were gay.

I pointed out that if you were gonna take some of the most important gay writers of the twentieth century—writers who happened to be gay, by the way—who were not activists, so to speak—you start with Proust, and Stein, and you work your way right up through to the present—with a lot, including Tennessee Williams, and many, many modern writers, poets—you'll find that the majority of them did not find their identity in being gay. They found their identity in being writers, one of whose shaping forces was the fact that they were gay. I made a lot of friends, and some enemies, at the Outwrite Conference. I remember that Paul Monette quite agreed with me, and some others did, too. My only objection was the fact there is the ghettoization, and the assumption that we're valued only because we are gay—and that therefore that must be our only subject—leads to ghettoization, and I thought that the whole thing was supposed to be an attempt toward assimilation.

SC: But aren't these gay writers motivated by a concern to create work that has an immediate political effect, in the sense that Shaw would have liked it?

EA: Political effect, fine, but you could be a writer who is gay and accomplish the same thing without writing about gay themes. You must not let the gayness become a limitation, and I find this happening a lot. There's an awful lot of good writing done by gay writers, but there's also a lot of *shit* being published, because there's a gay audience that will read it because it's by gay writers, and it's pushed by gay publishers. And that's the kind of thing that I don't like. I've never—never ever—made a secret about my sexual predilections. It seems to be one of the many, many things that I am. I'm a liberal Democrat, I live in the United States. I'm many things, and being gay is one of them. But it's not the defining thing in my life.

SC: Certainly. At the risk of jumping around, topically—

EA: Mmm, why not?

SC: I wanted to point to a couple of passages from Aristotle. Most of your work, and so much of modern drama, is very concerned with language. Aristotle is very clear when he says that language is secondary: "Plot is the heart and soul of drama." "The dramatist must construct action before words." What are we to make of the fact that drama seems to have gone through such a basic change?

EA: Well, I don't agree with your premise. Words are a conveyer of the emotional, intellectual message of the piece. Words are what is used to communicate. I don't find any worthwhile drama that has become about words. I've never put a speech in a play of mine just because I liked the sound of the language. I keep telling my students: "Anything you put in a play—any speech—has got to do one of two things: either define character or push the action of the play along. Otherwise, it should leave—it should go away."

SC: There's been a lot of concern about content restrictions in NEA grants, and several people have called for the abolition of the NEA. Would you prefer to see no public funding of the arts, or public funding that restricts content?

EA: I would rather have no public funding than censorship. But the whole question, after what's happened with the NEA, is so corrupt in its logic, and so corrupt in its reporting. What is being attempted is stripping the American people of aesthetic education. We're supposed to give people a twelfth-grade education in this country. I say that unless you give people an aesthetic education, you run the risk of raising highly educated barbarians. It's our responsibility to give them an aesthetic education at the same time, and that's one of the things that the NEA does—gives people an aesthetic education.

Approximately five percent of the money of the NEA ever goes to individual grants, by the way—individual creative people. Ninety-five percent of it goes to organizations which supply the forum for the intellectual argument to take place. People never think about *that,* either. There have been twenty-six thousand grants given by the NEA up to this point, of which I believe eleven or twelve have raised any question.

It has nothing to do with three Mapplethorpe photos of erect penises. It has nothing to do with that whatever. I saw that exhibition in Cincinnati, by the way. You could barely even see them because they were face up on a high table, and you had to lean over and you had to *look* at them. And they were tiny—and they were in a small room which said—you know—"Abandon all hope, ye who enter here." But then again, I have similar attitudes about people who feel that the flag should not be burned. I think this particular kind of *jingoism* is intolerable.

But the people who want to destroy the National Endowment for the Arts, and therefore destroy the aesthetic education of the people, are afraid of an aesthetically informed people. They're afraid of the kind of intelligent voting that might take place. They're afraid of the kind of rational discourse that might result from aesthetically educated people. They're *terrified* of the intellectual. They're terrified of the life of the mind, because they know that they're gonna end up out of office. It's pretty appalling, what's going on.

SC: It's very frightening, yes. You've talked about aesthetic education. People need a specific type of education to appreciate certain art.

EA: Well, it certainly helps, yes . . .

SC: How did the American public respond to *Box?*

EA: Well, you must remember that *Box* was done in context with *Quotations from Chairman Mao Tse-Tung,* though I have directed it myself, separately. Audiences who have experienced various kinds of theater are not put off by seeing a play in which there is nobody onstage, just a voice. They listen, and then they're quite interested in it.

SC: But don't they need to be prepared for it by having seen works like it?

EA: It would help, I suppose. I always go back and remember the report that when Beckett's play *Waiting for Godot* was done in San Quentin prison, in front of people who'd never seen a play before, the audience responded with comprehension and enthusiasm.

SC: But you can appreciate *Waiting for Godot* in naturalistic terms. Could people accept *Box* on its own terms, or did they need to have been prepared for it?

EA: I don't think you can ever be fully prepared for that which is startlingly new, nor should you expect to be. That's what television is based on, and most movies are based on—the redoing of the familiar. The best drama doesn't do that. *Box* was based, as far as I'm concerned, on a lot of Beckett's work. I thought it was a perfectly comprehensible experience to anybody who was willing to say: "This is the way this wants to be. Let's approach it on its terms rather than my preconditioning." Anybody who's unwilling to take that risk is not going to enjoy much theater at all.

SC: That's very tough, though. It's very tough to learn how to accept a work of art on its own terms. I don't know where we start.

EA: Well, I try to do it every time I look at a painting, every time I go to a play, an opera, a concert. Every time I go to a play, I say to myself: "All right. This is the first play I've ever seen." I'm not bringing any preconditions. I try to avoid any comparative stuff. I say: "Let it happen."

SC: But didn't the playwright stem from work that he'd seen in order to create that play?

EA: Well, I think most playwrights do a trick on themselves. They *have to* do a trick on themselves. We should be enormously informed as to the history of the art form we're looking at—completely informed. We should have done our homework. But at the same time, we should also, every time we sit down to write a play, write the first play that's ever been written. We are writing the first play that's ever been written. The audience should be seeing the first play that it has ever seen. If you have that particular kind of communication, then I think you have a fair chance.

A Playwright's Adventures
in the Visual Arts

1997

WHILE IT IS tempting to begin this article about a playwright's adventures in the visual arts with yet another critique of *Sensation* at The Royal Academy I shall refrain, for I have not yet seen the show in situ, though I know the work of most of the artists. The exhibit is clearly (and intentionally, I imagine) a wholeheartedly theatrical event, and I look forward to seeing it all on its present walls and to try to distinguish the art pieces themselves from their provocative context.

Plays, too, can seem quite different depending on circumstance, read rather than seen, free from either the distortion or the amplification of performance, and judged less as commerce than art.

I did not begin my life in the arts as a playwright, or as a writer of any kind. I drew and painted when I was very young— very young—and while all of what I did has disappeared, and while I am certain it was not very good, I recall a way with shading in the drawings and a very curious, perhaps outlandish color sense with paint.

In my twenties I took up painting again briefly—very briefly—working in a constructivist manner, as much as anything, I think, to sense what Malevich and Puni "felt" while they made their amazing art. I quit, quickly, when I realized I was feeling nothing beyond a certain curiosity that I was making imitations which, in some instances, looked, to my eye, every bit as good as the originals.

I grew up—an adopted child—in an upper-middle-class American household, the walls of which were hung with late nineteenth-century French paintings—lots of Bouguereau, I think, and probably a few wonderful (as I see it now) Rosa Bonheurs. I went away to boarding school at twelve and began festooning my walls with reproductions borrowed from the school library—Klee, Picasso, Arp, Miro. So much for home education.

I was writing by then—not plays though—and had begun to listen to classical music. I was probably at the beginnings of an understanding that all the arts relate, feed off of, amplify, and instruct one another, and that, no matter which of the arts we settle in to, it is folly to become so parochial that we are no longer eager to be nourished by the others.

This is particularly true for a playwright, for a playwright is the only writer whose work exists not only in words but, as importantly, as a heard and seen experience. A playwright who cannot "hear" is like a tone-deaf composer; a playwright who cannot "see" is like a weak-eyed or color-blind painter.

There are times when I am writing that I feel I am composing, and what I "see" as I write has the substance of the visual arts—with some of the complexity of slow dance thrown in.

The world is full of tone-deaf, half-blind playwrights, and, while they are never the very best, they can appeal to audiences with the same afflictions.

I don't know why I began being an accumulator of art (I reject the snobbish term "collector") but I think I must have looked at a painting by a certain young American artist one day—forty years ago?—and thought, "I think I would like to look at this painting longer than I can at the gallery; I think I would like to live with it." The artist was barely known, the painting was three hundred dollars, and I had begun. The artist is still barely known—he teaches in Virginia now—but I have the painting yet, and it is still worth looking at.

I am not a wealthy man (in a world filled with billionaires very few of us are) and I have always been willing (eager!) to take chances with emerging talent. Oh, back in the good old days I was able to acquire the work of world-famous artists for what is called a song—Arp, Schwitters, Chagall, Picasso, Moholy-Nagy—but once the ownership of art gave status to the status-conscious and art became very big business, all that changed.

I have accumulated, for the most part, over the forty years, the work of younger artists—American, British, German, Japanese— sculpture, painting, drawings, as well as an extensive holding of African works. I have never counted the number of works I possess (it must be a few hundred) and I have never bought to resell, but I have found that along with the "mistakes" (good artists who have fallen into the cracks) my "eye" has been fairly subtle and intelligent in a commercial sense.

I maintain an artists residency a hundred miles from New York City, a place where young writers and visual artists (no composers, alas, unless they can work away from the piano) can come and work for an extended period of time, free from economic pressure, a place where—most important—artists from different disciplines can relate to one another, learn from, instruct.

We choose our friends because we wish to be with them, to learn from, to be nurtured by. We should absorb art for the same reasons.

My taste in the visual arts tends to run to the nondecorative, the tough rather than the simply pleasing, the abstract rather than the pictorial, and I am drawn to that art which is about art—the Cubists, the Constructivists, the Bauhaus, Duchamp, Bueys, the Abstract Expressionists, and, constantly, to the young artists who stand at the edge of the cliff, look over, assume they can fly, jump, and, very often, discover that they are right.

As I think about my tastes in music and the visual arts I suspect it all is a piece with my playwriting—that how I "see" and how I "hear" determines how I think, and that determines how I write, and *that*, of course, determines who I am.

SPEECH TO THE AMERICAN COUNCIL FOR THE ARTS

1998

I LIKE BEING a playwright, which is fortunate, since that's one of the few things that I can do with any competence. And it is nice to be able to pass your life doing that which you feel that you might be doing with some competence, and possibly, possibly even communicating with a few people.

Because the function of the arts, is it not, is absolute communication. The function of the arts is to put us in greater contact with ourselves and with each other, to question our values, to question the status quo, to make us rethink that which we believe we believe.

One of the things that worries me so much about this civilization we call the United States—or at least Max Lerner was kind enough to call us a civilization—one of the things that worries me most about the civilization of the United States is whether or not we are one of these bizarre civilizations that may be on its way downhill before it has ever reached its zenith.

All civilizations have a duration. All civilizations have a period of enormous vitality, and then a kind of coasting status, and then eventually they began to subside, sometimes violently and sometimes merely with a whimper.

I worry sometimes that the American civilization may be on its way downhill.

I think one of the reasons that I concern myself, perhaps more than a number of other writers do, with the state of our societal and cultural health has to do with the time in our history that I became a functioning writer.

In the early 1960s in the Unites States, we believed that just about anything was possible. We had gone through the years of the Eisenhower nonpresidency. We had John Kennedy as our president. Youth, vitality, vigor, and the arts were burgeoning, at least in the major cities of the United States; they were vital and exciting.

In 1955, for example—and I looked this up—-of the four most performed playwrights in the United States, all of them were dead. Eight years later, of the four most performed playwrights in the United States, three of them were living playwrights.

At the time I sort of emerged on the scene, the paperback book market had come into existence in the United States. People were able to get finally for very little money not only the classic works of world literature, but also the avant-garde works from Europe and Asia and the United States.

People began going to concerts of serious contemporary music. Finally there were more people sitting in the audience at these concerts than there were performing onstage.

Museums and galleries were beginning to show the work of tough young artists, and people were looking, and people were paying attention.

It was an enormously exciting time to be involved in the arts in the United States.

And in this period, for reasons that I like to think were rational—but perhaps were merely accident—the National Endowment for the Arts was born.

We guarantee people in this country a twelfth-grade education. I am convinced that the National Endowment for the Arts was created in the understanding that, unless we provide and aesthetic education for the people of this country, we are not doing our job; that unless we provide an aesthetic education for the people, we will be raising a society of informed barbarians.

And so the National Endowment for the Arts was born, pouring millions and ultimately hundreds of millions of dollars into the aesthetic education of people of this country.

The attempt recently on the part of the Congress of the United States to dismantle and ultimately destroy the National Endowment for the Arts, to destroy the aesthetic education of people of this country, worries me greatly because it tells me far more than I am comfortable to know about the state of our moral, philosophical, psychological, and ethical health; because these people who are voting to destroy the aesthetic education of the people of this country are doing it because we as a society have put them in the positions of power to do it.

So it is not their fault; it is ours.

There is a good and a bad side to everything. Two steps forward, one step back, usually, in a participatory democracy, though I wonder sometimes how participatory a democracy are we.

In this last election, forty-nine percent of the electorate voted, which means that you and I are being governed by the will of approximately twenty-four and a half of the potential electorate.

This is not participatory democracy. It is a kind of reverse elitism, and this worries me greatly as well.

Do we care so little—do we care so little about how we are governed that we don't even bother to take care to see that we are governed rationally and intelligently?

Have we become so passive a society? Are we indeed dying in life? Have we become so passive that we will lose this enormously fragile thing called democracy?

I travel around a lot, and have, over the years. And over the years I have spent a lot of time—especially in the bad old days before the collapse of the Soviet Union—in Eastern Europe. I have spent time in other totalitarian societies as well.

But I spent a lot of time in the old Soviet Union going back to 1963, when John Steinbeck was kind enough to drag me along when he was part of the cultural exchange program. And he was asked, bring a young American writer with you; and John took me.

Over the years I have been to the Soviet Union with a number of writers I admire, including Bill Styron. He and I spent time together in Moscow.

Arthur Miller and I have spent a lot of time carrying placards, marching in front of the Soviet Cultural Ministry and the UN delegation in New York to protest the arrest of the writers and other people who dare disagree with their government in the Soviet Union.

So I have spent a lot of time in totalitarian societies, which has probably made me even more worried about the passivity of the United States than I would be without that particular information.

The first time I went to the Soviet Union, I met a lot of people, dissident writers, quasi-dissident writers, and also the cultural commissars, the people who decided at that time what frame of reference the Soviet citizen would have to contemplate reality, who decided which novelists would have their novels published in editions of two million, and which novelists would be sent to slave labor camps; who decided which painters would have their paintings exhibited in the Tretyakov Museum in Moscow, and which ones, if they dared having an open-air exhibit of abstract painting on the banks of the Moscow River, would see the tanks come and bulldoze their paintings into the river; the cultural commissars who decided which composers would have cushy jobs at the conservatories and which ones, if their music was too adventuresome, would find themselves out of work: the people who decided what consciousness the Soviet citizen was able to develop.

One of the young writers that I met in my first visit to the Soviet Union was a young man named Andre Amalrik. He eventually spent several years in a Soviet jail for having written a book called *Will the Soviet Union Survive Until 1984?*

He was not far off.

He is dead now, alas. After he was finally thrown out of the Soviet Union, he was killed, very oddly, one midnight in northern Spain on a lonely road. He was on his way to monitor the Soviet noncompliance with the Helsinki Accords.

Back in 1963, he and I met on a snowy night in Moscow and spent a long time talking. And one of the things that he put forward to me was a theory he had that it was the intention of the people who ran the culture in his country to create what he referred to as a semantic collapse between our cultures, to create a situation where it would be impossible for communication really to exist, a total breakdown of language, a total breakdown of intention and of semantics.

Well, I had done my homework. I had read my George Orwell. I knew what he was talking about. But it was interesting to hear it in the mouth of the lion, so to speak.

I went back to England a few weeks later and began to think of it, about what Amalrik had told me. And I began to wonder.

This semantic collapse that he was talking about, was this possible only between two such different societies as the United States and the Soviet Union, or wasn't it as least theoretically possible that there could be an ultimate and total breakdown even in the United States between those tough truths the intellectuals and the creative artists wished to tell the people about themselves, and that which the people of the United States were willing to listen to?

And then it occurred to me even more—and it is a feeling that has been growing in me all of these years—that, yes, such a semantic collapse in the United States is not only possible, but I fear that it is occurring more and more. I find that we are in the middle of this particular kind of semantic collapse, and it worries me greatly.

Mind you, I would rather be a writer in the United States than in any other country I know of. And I have been to a lot of countries, and I have seen what creative people have to put up with.

The hostility, the occasional hostility, the occasional intentional misunderstanding of one's work, the occasional dismissal of one's work in the United States, is nothing, nothing compared to the literal life-and-death matter of daring to write the truth in a totalitarian society.

We are children compared to what other people have to put up with. I have seen creative people in totalitarian societies risk their very lives to read a book.

We don't do that in this country.

There is in this country yet no one to tell us, no, you may not read that book; no, you may not listen to that string quartet; no, you may not look at that painting; no, you may not read that poem; no, you may not see that play; no, you may not read that magazine or that newspaper.

There is nobody in the United Stated yet to deny us access to the metaphor, if you will, access to the education that the arts can give us in this country; no one except ourselves.

The self-censorship, the abdication of participation on the part of so many people in the United States, is a form of death in life. It is a form of not participating fully in one's own life. It is indeed a form of death in life.

Of course people can easily say, so what? What does it really matter? Here he is running on about the responsibility of people to the arts. Haven't we had a rather rough twenty-five years or so in the United States? Haven't we had the presidency disgraced by Mr. Nixon? Have we not had the fabric of our society torn part by the war in Vietnam?

Have we not had younger people for many years now turning off from voting, turning off from participating politically in our society?

We are the only democracy that I know of where the college-age students are not at the involved, informed political forefront.

We live enormously dangerously as a society. Our economy, as a result of eight years of the Reagan disastrous mismanagement, gives the false illusion of being a healthy economy.

Many things have been going wrong in this country. So why should we concern ourselves with anything so unimportant as the relationship between the arts and the rest of the people of this country?

Well, I can give you a couple of reasons why I think we should. One of them has to do with what it is that distinguishes us from all the other animals.

If there are a few creationists among you, I hope you will forgive that word "other." But there it is.

There is something that distinguishes us from all the other animals. It used to be thought for a long time that we were the only animal that could efficiently use tools. But the more we began to look around us, we discovered that other animals could use tools just as efficiently as we did—but nowhere near as destructive of course; there are not very, very many animals who use weapons to kill their own kind.

We are one of the very, very few that has managed that advance in civilization.

It was thought for a long time that perhaps we were the only animal capable of constructing and maintaining a complex society. But the more we began to look around and see the societies of termites, of ants, bees, and other creatures, we saw that they were capable of maintaining a society at least as complex as that of Mainland China, and perhaps not as cruel.

It was thought for a while that perhaps we were the only animal possessed of—what is it called?—an immortal soul.

Well, whenever I hear that, I am reminded of the remark that I hope is not apocryphal, made by a—I can't remember who it is— late-nineteenth-century French Catholic novelist, who said, if I may not be with my dog in heaven, I will not go.

And those of us who have passed so much of our lives in the company of Irish wolfhounds know that the concept of the soullessness of other animals is preposterous nonsense.

Let me give you what I consider to be the one thing that really does distinguish us from all the other animals. And it is simply this:

We are the only animal who consciously and intentionally creates art. We are the only animal who has invented the metaphor, the arts, to define consciousness to ourselves, to define ourselves to ourselves. We are the only one that does this.

Now, I know about all of these experiments that have been made for the past twenty years with gorillas and chimpanzees, our persuading ourselves that they wish to be communicated with by language and that we are capable of doing it.

They figured out soon—quite soon—that gorillas and chimpanzees—all female, by the way—that the only gorillas and chimpanzees who even wanted to think about talking to us were female. I have no idea what this means.

But it was soon discovered that they did not wish to communicate vocally. They wished to use their vocal chords for far more sensible things like shrieking and screaming and yelling.

But a number of these female chimpanzees and gorillas were willing to learn a kind of sign language with us, to communicate with us by sign.

Some of them, I am told, some of these lady chimpanzees and gorillas, have developed a vocabulary in excess of five hundred words. This is certainly a far larger vocabulary than that of many people I have met in New York City.

But to my knowledge, with this vocabulary—and certainly a vocabulary that a number of playwrights I know find sufficient to write with—as far as I know, none of these lady chimpanzees or gorillas has yet written a play.

Now, I am sure that as soon as one does, given the state of our theater, it will be performed on Broadway at once. And given the state of our majority criticism, it will probably run for four and a half years, since our theater audiences, at least in the major commercial arenas, go to the theater merely when they are told to, not because it is something they think they might possibly learn something from.

But until this first lady chimpanzee or gorilla writes this first play and I get to have a chance to talk to her, for which I will be happy to learn sign language, and she convinces me that she did it on purpose—it was not monkey on the keyboard, so to speak—I hold that we are the only animal who has invented and uses art as a method to communicate ourselves to ourselves.

And I am convinced that this has a great deal to do with evolution; again, my apologies to the creationists.

I was very happy to read that the pope has decided there may be something to this whole theory of evolution.

I am convinced that the invention of the metaphor, the invention of art, if you will, is part of the evolutionary process.

We all used to have a tail, you know. Well, it wasn't one gigantic community tail. That would be very restricting. But we all used to have our own tails. There is—take it on faith—at the base of your spine a little jut of bone called the coccyx, I believe. This is the vestigial remnant of your tails.

Now, to simplify only slightly, I think this is what happened: somewhere along the line, our tails fell off and we developed art. We developed the need and the ability to be able to hold an accurate mirror up to ourselves, to observe ourselves, to observe our behaviors, to observe our intentions; and therefrom came the evolutionary development of art.

And we live in one of the few civilizations, one of the few societies where we are permitted to practice evolution without cavil and without restraint.

As I said, there are no commissars sitting on top of us, saying you may not do this.

But the particular kind of censorship of our own self-awareness and self-knowledge that we tolerate and permit is shocking and makes me worry greatly about our civilization.

Democracy is enormously fragile. Other countries have learned this, that democracy that is not participated in fully and totally is in great danger.

I was pleased, if slightly surprised, to read this morning in the *Chicago Tribune* an article agreeing with some of my theories, an article which suggested that our passivity, our lack of sense of responsibility to ourselves and to our fellows, is dangerous and destructive to democracy in the United States.

The late Diana Trilling, in one of her last utterances, remarked that we no longer have rational discourse, rational angry discourse in the United States.

She may have been talking about something that went out the window when her husband died. And while I do not wish to bring Lionel Trilling back from the grave, nor Diana Trilling for that matter, I think she had something there.

We do not have rational contentious discourse in the United States. The last time we had a political debate on the national level in the United States, a free-wheeling debate where the candidates were permitted to question each other, to talk without interruption and without stage management, was in 1960 in the debates between Kennedy and Nixon.

The rest have been stage managed. The rest have been controlled to the extent that we learn absolutely nothing about the humanity or even the ideas of our candidates. We tend to vote more often because the spin doctors tell us how we reacted before we have had the opportunity to react ourselves.

It is part of the growing and continuing passivity of us as a society. The middle-browing, if you will, of American culture is the result of commercial need, and absolutely nothing else.

It is not a democratizing of culture in the United States. It is the mass cultural selling.

We hear terrible terms of approbation these days, like elitist, liberal, thinking.

Worry about it. Worry a good deal about it.

BETTY PARSONS

A CONVERSATION WITH EDWARD ALBEE, JONATHAN THOMAS, AND ANNE COHEN DEPIETRO

1998

DePietro: Clearly, Betty's reputation as a dealer overwhelmed her own career as an artist. I know that you and she were good friends. Did you know of her work before her death? Did she talk to you about it?

Albee: Oh sure. For example, I was at that Montclair show; and she was there. I knew her work maybe even before I met her. But I don't remember—I've never in my life remembered when I've met anybody, how long I've known them, where I've met them, or when I've seen their work first, so it's very hard for me to answer these questions. I knew Betty for a long time. Why sure, I knew the work before she died, of course. In fact I acquired that piece in there before she died.

DePietro: You acquired the construction from her?

Albee: Oh yes.

DePietro: Did she ever speak to you about any frustrations she might have had in terms of showing her own work, in terms of being overwhelmed by her reputation as a dealer or by the artists in her stable?

Albee: No, I don't have that feeling. Of course, she was a quite private person, and shy, and not given to blowing her own horn. No, I would never say that she was. She may have denigrated it as her hobby. She loved it and she did it very seriously, and she liked it a lot. I didn't care much for her work until she turned relatively abstract, after all that stuff from the twenties, you know. . . .

DePietro: The early work is a little uneven, by comparison . . .

Albee: It is, but she suddenly found herself . . .

DePietro: Around 1947, bingo . . .

Albee: I imagine she was helped by the artistic environment she was working in, you know, it "fed" her. The interesting thing about Betty's work is—you can't always tell necessarily whether an artist's work is his own—but I could always see a work by Betty fifty yards away, and I'd know instantly, it's Betty's.

DePietro: Why?

Albee: There's something highly individual about it. I never confuse it with anybody else. I'm not talking about the early stuff now; I'm talking especially about the constructions and the paintings. I always know it's Betty's. It's not true of everybody, you know. A lot of abstract expressionists were less distinctive, especially the second-generation ones: "Isn't that what's his name, isn't that so-and-so?"

DePietro: They can all sort of fall together.

Albee: They can. But I found Betty's work enormously pleasing.

DePietro: I think there's a great spontaneity to her work. I'm presuming she must have worked with tremendous haste because she was so prolific. She traveled so much and she was clearly so active in the gallery. She wore so many hats.

Albee: Well, she had to get out of the city. I think she did most of her paintings—I could be wrong about that—but I think she did them up on the North Fork, because she worked so hard there. There's a wonderful photograph somewhere of Betty sitting in her studio up there, just surrounded by pieces of wood and half-constructed things. It's a wonderful sort of thing, maybe you can find it in Lee Hall's book.

DePietro: Bill Rayner has some photographs of Betty walking along the beach, working and assembling some of her constructions. . . .

Albee: I know some of those photographs. Let me get Jonathan in here—that's going to be helpful. . . . This is Jonathan Thomas.

DePietro: Was Parsons frustrated at the lack of opportunity to show her work or was that not important to her?

Albee: I don't know if it was important, but she didn't go around griping. How she may have felt very privately about it, I don't know. I knew she was sort of awkward about it, dismissive: "Oh, yeah, I did that." I think she cared a lot, though.

DePietro: I know that in the statement you very kindly wrote for us, you referred to her world as being rather brutal. Is that in terms of dealing, which can at times be rather cutthroat?

Albee: Oh, of course. There's an awful lot of backbiting going on.

DePietro: Esteban Vicente recently was telling me stories about his life, about his friendships with Dalí and Luis Buñuel and Picasso, and in between a little bit about Betty, and he remarked, "Ah, she was no dealer, she was an artist!"

Albee: Well, she kept saying, I won't show anybody whose work I really don't like a lot, and she was always talking about all of her artists, her major artists, her minor artists, with enthusiasm and detail. She would follow you around from painting to painting and talk about the work. She bubbled with enthusiasm.

DePietro: I've been wondering about Betty's work in terms of any possible relationship to her place in Southold that she loved so much. Do you think there's any connection that you can see to her work thematically or in any other respect with Long Island? The titles are allusive, certainly. And the materials came from the beach, but beyond that, I'm trying to . . .

Albee: Well, I know she was happy there. There was a special light, and then a quality of "thing" there. She was happy there. And some of the drawings were of course influenced by what's-his-name—the earlier American guy who did seascapes.

Thomas: If she was in a spot for a period of time she was influenced by it visually because she was always out there looking and she always was working. That woman was always working and she always had her paints. We went down to St. Martin to stay with her, and you know, I wanted to go and lie on the beach, and Betty wanted to paint. And the same up there in Southold. It was constant work, always something going on, and she would have everybody involved, too. I mean in St. Martin, Paul Taylor would be down on the beach picking up wood, Jasper Johns would pick up wood for her. All of these people would say, "Oh, you'd better take this back for Betty."

Albee: And it was kind of, "If Betty doesn't want it then Louise [Nevelson] will."

Thomas: That was the interesting thing. We were good friends with Louise Nevelson and we were also good friends with Lee Krasner and we were also good friends with Betty Parsons. And we could not see any of these women in the same room. So I wonder about the art world and women. I mean you've got women dealers not showing very many female artists. And if females do not show . . .

DePietro: It's said that Betty showed the work of more women artists than any other gallery in New York.

Thomas: Until she had a falling out with Agnes Martin. And I don't know what that was all about. They had a really big falling out. And every time I would talk to Lee [Krasner] about showing with Betty, then Lee would say I don't know what she does.

Albee: Well that's because Betty was ignoring Lee for her husband.

Thomas: That's what happened. Of course that was happening. And Lee referred to Louise as "Luigi" and Louise Nevelson would refer to Lee Krasner as "The Widow" or "The Weedless Widow" or something like that. It was fun. And it was really remarkable how they held these grudges to the end.

Albee: One of the most interesting things about Betty was that she showed so many of these interesting artists early in their careers, not like dealers today who buy and show artists' estates.

DePietro: You did make that point, or you alluded to it, that she showed them before they were famous, and once they became tremendously well-known they went over to Janis, who marketed them more aggressively.

Albee: But it's interesting, aesthetically, as far as Betty's eye, the freshness of the new talent was what interested her. I don't know what kind of businesswoman she was, she may have sold things for too little money, but who's to say, to please these artists. But she cared about artists early on, in the freshness of their careers, that's what's important.

Thomas: But she'd also get caught in the spirit of the artists, she'd see something . . .

DePietro: I know it's been said, too, at least in Lee Hall's book, that once her big artists left, Lee implied that she was more content showing the work of lesser-known artists because she wouldn't get caught up in egos and things.

Albee: Well, she did get stung a couple of times. But I would suspect that's as much conjecture as anything.

Thomas: I think that she was really attracted to the energy of kids starting out, that she really liked that energy, that she liked being around them, that she liked discovering things with them. She was still, in her eighties, discovering things.

Albee: She might have been undercut by the awfulness of the art-dealing world too, you know. She might not have wanted to play those games.

DePietro: Do you think that she was at all derivative in her own work?

Albee: The earlier work I found quite derivative. That's why I wish I could remember the name of one of the artists who did wonderful drawings of the shores and sea in books of America in the twenties and she . . . I don't remember . . . It doesn't matter. . . . Anyway, the early work I found quite derivative, sure.

DePietro: And what about her abstractions?

Albee: I don't find them derivative, that's why I find them so interesting, that's why I can always say, "That is a Betty Parsons." I don't confuse it with anybody.

DePietro: I think, again, that it was probably Lee Hall who talked about how, . . . somewhere I've read about how influenced she was by some of her artists . . . who did she mention? Ad Reinhardt, maybe?

Albee: Early Reinhardt, yes.

DePietro: I particularly like her work from the fifties, in which there are these auras of complementary colors around the forms, and they're especially radiant. And more than anything, I think the titles are allusive to her years on Long Island.

Albee: Well she called this something . . .

DePietro: *Fog and the Sea* . . .

Albee: *Fog and the Sea* . . .

DePietro: And that, to me, is very evocative.

Albee: Yeah.

DePietro: I think it's a particularly lovely one.

Albee: Well, I was thinking, the way Betty worked, she didn't feel the pressure to be commercial, successful, to be trendy, or even to sell. I mean, she painted, she did her constructions, for herself, fundamentally, because that's what she did; that's who she was, which I think allowed her this individuality which I find so strong in her later work. I mean so many artists now watch things, and think, "Can I do that, and is that going to be all right to do? What's the next trend and all the rest of the stuff." Somebody who is trying to catch the brass ring. It's sad.

DePietro: That's true.

Albee: Because it's too late to figure it out. But I never thought that Betty felt competitive, let's put it that way. Maybe she did. One thing that stands out in my long life is that artists—and

I've known all sorts of people—Mark Rothko used to visit me out here, for example, and I've known an awful lot of people in the arts, and we don't sit around and talk about the arts. We don't do it. I mean the closest that Mark ever got to talking about the arts with me was when he saw something by Avery at my place, or how interested he was by Avery, but we didn't sit around and talk about that stuff. So Betty and I would never talk about those aspects that everybody's so interested in.

DePietro: And no one will ever know. I wonder why that is.

Albee: I suppose we never wanted to talk business.

Thomas: Betty didn't talk; Betty wasn't a big storyteller. How could she be with all those other talkers. Betty would be just working, or doing something. (Albee: Well, she talked occasionally.) She was always quick, enthusiastic to do anything about art.

DePietro: She worked incessantly.

Albee: But do you think Betty ever seemed competitive?

Thomas: Competitive as an artist? I never saw, I can't remember her ever saying anything really mean about other artists, or putting them down. She was always pretty positive about her showing some individuals, and sometimes that would get her in trouble. She wasn't "P.C.," she'd be politically incorrect.

DePietro: Why do you think her work hasn't really received the recognition it deserves? When she died, her collection was grabbed up by institutions. Only a couple of her works on paper went into museum collections, but the Foundation has most of her paintings. No one seems to have wanted them. The constructions have found their way around a little bit more, into more private rather than public collections, but what do you think it is, that she has never . . . ?

Albee: I do think it has something to do with the attitude that, here was this rich girl, society girl, had a gallery, and oh, she painted too. That's the prevalent attitude, alas.

Thomas: Maybe the timing of some of the work.

Albee: I admired the work a lot. I think it's very, very good.

DePietro: Is there anything else that either of you would like to address in terms of Betty's own work, opportunity, lack thereof, sources of inspiration, anything I'm not thinking of at the moment?

Albee: Give us another couple of hours.

Mrs. de Menil's Liquor Closet

1999

IF YOU ARE a collector of art—or an "accumulator," as many more of us are or prefer to be called, as we find the term "collector" pretentious—you have doubtless accumulated works both large and small and of varying economic clout.

Well, the above may not be quite true: You may have a thing for "big art"—huge paintings, say, or room-size sculpture—or be weird about assembling only postcard-size drawings, or believe that dollar signs must be visible on anything on your walls— usually the embarrassing product of a "collection" assembled for the newly rich and newly art aware by a dealer—or you "take chances," which usually means accumulating "new" art by "new" people, the majority of which, unless your eye is remarkable, will end up sooner or later in the garage with the discarded washing machine.

No. Most of us who accumulate art are given to variety and have large and small paintings, drawings, prints, large and small sculpture—whatever. And since the big pieces look best in the big rooms, you are (unless you've figured out, of course, that the right big painting looks super right next to the right small one) stuck with the problem of what to do with the twenty or so small paintings and drawings that don't fit in.

And the one thing you don't want to do—if you really care about art—is embarrass the small art pieces by putting them in the bathrooms, say, or narrow upstairs halls, far away from the blockbusters, as if they were minor because small.

Another unhappy decision is to relegate the small pieces to the summer residence, where everything, including taste, is more informal.

These are not happy solutions. But what *do* you do with these small artworks?

A rich friend of mine, a man of exquisite taste and unlimited funds, had assembled his own small traveling museum. He had suitcases built—properly slotted wood-lined leather—in which he put small framed paintings and drawings, and he took them with him wherever he went: to the Plaza Athénée in Paris, the Connaught in London, country estates when he went visiting for weekends. When he arrived, he would remove whatever (usually decorator) art was on the walls and put up his own traveling collection, having cleared it with the management, of course.

It made him feel more at home, he said, and it made visiting him when he traveled pure pleasure.

The de Menil family of Houston, Texas—from France originally—wealthy from the oil industry, came up with a double solution to the problem, a public one and a private one, and those of us who have experienced both are grateful for both.

First, you build a museum! And you make sure it's one of the finest privately accomplished museums in the United States.

I teach playwriting at the University of Houston each spring, and at least once a week I go to this museum, just to wander about, revisiting "old friends" in the various departments—an African mask, an Oceanic figure I'd steal if it weren't so big and if I weren't so nice, a Northwest Coast Indian object, and entire rooms of spectacularly wonderful pieces from the twentieth-century collection.

A word here to the ambitious: Don't start a museum unless your taste is impeccable, for you will be judged by museums of this quality and elegance.

Second, have Philip Johnson build a house for you, a house where the rest of your art lives and breathes organically and unobtrusively. I've been to this house often, and never once have I felt "subjected" to the splendid art; it is there where it is; it belongs where it is, and you have a feeling all is right with the world.

Still . . . what to do with some of the other stuff? Some small pieces just don't "work" in the overall design. Well, it's so simple—if you're a de Menil. Put them in a space almost everybody will go to from time to time—the room where the nourishment of conviviality is kept: the Liquor Closet.

Such a simple, such an elegant solution. You go to the Liquor Closet to get yourself a drink (and the hosts are happy to *let* you), and there you are face-to-face with a small Braque, a Victor Brauner, a Chagall, a Laurens, an Anne Ryan, a Schwitters. They are there with other pieces and with glasses and liquor bottles and stuff.

The only problem with this solution is that someday someone is going to be so happy with the art and the liquor that a permanent house guest will have been born.

I suppose every good idea has its downside.

CONTEXT IS ALL

EXCERPTS FROM A CONVERSATION WITH JONATHAN THOMAS AND HARRY RAND

2000

The following conversation with Harry Rand took place on the occasion of Albee's selection of nine sculptors, who appeared in From Idea to Matter.

HR: I want to get some of the show's assumptions made explicit. Did Ted Potter [Director of Anderson Gallery] put any constraints on you on who you would choose, or how to choose them?

EA: No, of course not. He knows my taste. He knows the work of some of the artists in the show. He knows the kind of work that I like. I don't know whether he's seen catalogues of previous exhibits that I've curated or not. He may have over the years.

No, no constraints. I imagine if I wanted to exhibit a piece which blew up the museum, he might have had a couple of reservations, though I understand that he wants a new one, so perhaps not.

HR: When you selected these artists, did you choose them with the idea that they might hang well together?

EA: Well, certainly not that they would be contradictory, nor was I after the trendy, which I'm opposed to greatly. The work is abstract, all abstract, all is hands-on work: very specifically, the artists' hands are very visible in all of the work. It strikes me—it's all art about art, about the definition of art.

HR: Yes, which is not at all the same as "art for art's sake." This is art aiming to advance the scope of human understanding, to mention things heretofore not remarked upon, to record or make an incident formerly beneath notice.

In looking over the art, what struck me was that, for an artist who works as you do, there might be a craving for the autographic art: the record of a touch and the art of the touch, as opposed to the precarious position of your work, which you send out into the world, and the plastic imagery is left to directors and actors.

EA: Well, I've never believed that, you see. I don't believe that is the way theater should be going. As a playwright, I started off wanting to be a composer and a visual artist when I was very young. I started doing paintings and drawings when I was quite young. And I discovered Mozart and Bach when I was eleven, so I decided I wanted to be a composer. But I failed in those two very, very quickly and very completely.

But being a playwright, you're not only a literary artist, but you're a visual artist, and you're a composer. It's an auditory experience and a visual experience, as well as a literary experience. So, as a playwright, I'm very involved in all three of those things, and I've learned probably as much as any layman knows about classical music over the years, and I know the literature very, very well. And with the visual arts, I started being very interested in the visual arts when I was going to school; I was renting reproductions of Kandinsky and Malevich and those people for my walls when I was fourteen and fifteen years old. So I've been very interested in the visual arts and became fairly knowledgeable in those. And I think that's helpful to a playwright, but also that's just my nature. I like those things: literature, and painting and sculpture, and music a lot. They all relate to me very much.

HR: If you see yourself as creating a continuum with the words and music and plastic imagery implicit on the page . . .

EA: No, what I said was, that I think for a playwright not to have the sensibility for musical composition and the visual arts is a limitation for him. I do think, when I'm writing a play, sometimes I'm writing a string quartet. I'm aware of the sound and the aesthetic similarities. But the visual thing is a little more remote; we do have a set, we do have an environment, and I'm very specific about the background I'd like for the plays. We have objects, sculptural objects, standing in position and moving, rather in the way that we would have in dance. It helps, I think, if you're going to be talking to lighting designers and set designers, it helps to have some awareness. I'm more interested always in dance setting than in the usual dramatic setting, unless you have the naturalistic play like *Virginia Woolf* where I want a cluttered living room.

HR: Do you think it works the other way? Do you think these artists have implicit in their work rhythms and cadences that are like speech and like drama?

EA: No, I wouldn't go that far. I've never thought of it in those terms. No, I'm not trying to relate any of this work to my work. That's not the intention of this show.

HR: I didn't know if it was, but I wanted to know if . . .

EA: Oh, goodness, no. No, no. I would imagine that my affection for the work helped determine my choices. I wouldn't like it so much unless I'd felt an aesthetic, not similarity, but congeniality. I don't know that one would go to see this show and say, "That's Edward Albee's mind there." Maybe, to a certain extent, but more his taste.

HR: I was thinking of the "wrong end of the telescope" sensation, where you can start with words and unpack from that rhythms and cadences and music, and therefore dance arises and therefore plastic imagery. . . .

EA: I think you'd be stretching it too far. I think you'd be constructing a case that might have validity, but it's beside the point here.

HR: That may account for your success as a playwright, whereas a visual artist might see the world in the visual, including all of those other—not necessarily synesthetic, but compacted and analogous—sensations.

EA: Yeah. But I don't want you to be coming to the conclusion that I like this work only because it relates to the way I work or I think.

HR: Not at all.

EA: The work is so dissimilar. It's the way I feel about sculpture. Now, obviously I'm not going to have any work that I'm not sympathetic to, right? Of course not.

HR: And there are deep sympathies.

EA: Yeah. There's a lot of stuff you can admire and not be

sympathetic to, and a lot of stuff you can be sympathetic to that you don't much admire. It's nice to be able to put the two of them together.

HR: Right, that's an adult sensibility and also a professional sensibility. The public doesn't generally understand the difference between the good and what you like.

EA: No, of course not, no. Well, the trick is that you should like what's good.

HR: There's certainly a historical pedigree for this kind of work. No one starts off from scratch with this. It's intelligent work.

EA: Oh, everybody comes from somebody. You have to come from somebody.

HR: Picasso had a great line about that, that you probably know. He said something like: "In life, it's not considered an honor not to have a father. Why should it be in art?"

EA: Exactly, yes.

HR: There's a lot of history and memory in these pieces.

EA: And that's something very interesting about Picasso, by the way, and I think someday people are going to realize how much more important his sculpture is than a lot of people do now. Because I think he didn't really do a painting that mattered much after about 1932, and a lot of the sculpture after that is wonderful.

HR: Yeah. Starting in the 1920s, when he rethinks abstraction, he becomes a different artist, and I think the two bodies of his work are underrated.

EA: It actually began in that period of 1931 and 1932 when he was doing the figures on the beach which he ended up doing as sculptures. That's a very interesting transition.

HR: That starts 1927–29. I think the sculptures and the lino cuts are two underrated bodies of work. Everyone thinks the linocuts are unimportant because kids do linoleum cut prints at camp, so how important can they be. But the linocuts of the 1950s really unite his visual virtuosity with the clarity of graphic device.

EA: I love his sculpture a lot.

HR: Are the artists in the show artists you personally collect?

EA: Yeah, but then again, that's hardly a limitation, since I have a lot of stuff. Do I have work by all these people? Yeah, sure. I have two pieces of John Duff's that are from 1972, early fiberglass wall pieces. I've known some of these artists, John Duff and Mia Westerlund Roosen and Richard Nonas, for a very long time. And Jonathan Thomas a long time, too. But some of them are like John Beech, whose work I became aware of in San Francisco about ten years ago, when he was a very young artist out there. David Fulton is a Houston artist. Barry Goldberg is working very quietly in Brooklyn; no one pays any attention to him, which is too bad. David McDonald is a West Coast artist also, whose work I saw out there. And Paul Whiting was a core fellow down at the University of Houston four years ago.

HR: Are you an inveterate gallery-goer?

EA: Yes, I go to galleries constantly, all the time.

HR: And did you see these pieces in your gallery explorations or do they represent recommendations from friends?

EA: I go to studios, too. It's very interesting, in that I see things hang in a way that most people don't usually see them. I remember back in 1940-something, I went to the then Museum of Nonobjective Art.

HR: What is now the Guggenheim Museum in New York.

EA: Before it was the Guggenheim. It was on Fifty-second or

Fifty-third Street, between Park and Madison on the second floor, run by Hilla Rebay at that time. And the sculptor who did *The Endless House*, Frederick Keisler, had hung a show there, and almost everything was just a foot above the floor. It was very interesting to see.

HR: It's a way to break through the visitor's complacency. You start thinking about space, which is what sculpture is all about: to make you think about space.

EA: And I think things should be hung up near the ceiling and on the floor and odd places.

HR: As long as you can make the sculpture be sensible.

EA: Yeah, that's right. But the stuff having to be at a level where people have to see it either sitting down or standing is very strange to me.

HR: It's literally a kind of pedestrian view of things.

EA: I mean, stuff that's meant to be on the floor, you can only put it on the floor. Or if it's small enough, on a table. But if it's very small and wants to be on the floor and doesn't want to be on the table, you put it on the floor.

HR: And there have been problems about that. When Anthony Caro was trying to figure out how to do the table pieces, the only thing he could think of to make them ultimately only table pieces was to have something, some element of the work, hanging off, and then it could only be a table piece. And of course the Richard Serra pieces you can leave on the floor, and the Andre pieces, using weight and gravity in different ways.

I have a personal theory that sculptors mature a lot later than painters. It takes a lot longer to make each individual sculpture, so it takes longer to make your first five thousand mistakes, but in general if—and this is my premise—painters come into their own and really mature at forty, sculptors generally do it around sixty. Not that I intend that this man should suffer ignominiously until he's sixty, but they hit their stride later on.

EA: Well, some painters, too, of course. Mark Rothko never sold a painting until he was in his fifties.

HR: Barnett Newman really didn't have his first show until he was almost forty, but that was a different time.

EA: Well, here's one—you can ask him about his work.

HR: Jonathan Thomas? [who has just entered the room]

EA: Yeah.

HR: No, I want to ask the curator.

EA: What are you putting in the show, the totems? About thirty-five of the totems?

HR: Would you ever know that a mathematician made these?

EA: Yeah, Jonathan Thomas studied pure mathematics in Canada.

HR: I'd like to ask each of you the same question, since we do have the luxury of having the artist and the curator in the same room, and that is: Do you have a preference for seeing these in larger or smaller masses of groupings?

EA: They're totally different in their effect.

JT: No, as far as I'm concerned, the piece is thirty pieces.

EA: I think he's relating it to what Louise Nevelson said to me about her stuff once: Louise said: "Every piece I've ever done is part of a big piece." And then when she did Mrs. N.'s Palace we saw exactly what she meant by that. Everything was knitting, also. Stitching, she meant everything was stitching.

JT: When people put together groups of three or five, it's fine, but, you know, I'd love thirty, since I think that's complete.

EA: I was helping to put together a show that Jonathan had in Chicago at Roy Boyd's Gallery a couple of years ago, and he had several groups of fifteen, seventeen, but there was one little niche that was very interesting: I took three of the smaller ones, one white one, and two black ones, and put them on a stand this high from the floor, of the taller white one and the two black ones in a little niche all by themselves, and it's a totally different effect. They work in small groups.

JT: I like other people interacting with work and putting groups together. I like that.

HR: When you see the large aggregates, you get two sensations; at least, I get two sensations. One of them is that there's a sculptural statement being made, a commitment to a specific rhythmic cadence, but the other one is that there's that sensation of seeing a cultural statement that only time and aggregation can produce. Like when you go to see these Dogon sites in Africa or indeed any culture, where you get this affirmation time and time again, and you get that commitment. And it's something that's lacking from a lot of modern art, where the single statement is supposed to carry all that weight, all that cultural weight, rather than committing to repetition and really make a very definite commitment. I realize that I'm using that word twice, but . . .

EA: Jonathan relates a lot of his work to the nonanthropomorphic, to geometry and pure mathematics.

JT: Well, when I started out, I thought I was doing a visual representation of the hypertext, because I kind of wanted it to go over and lead every thing; every sequence of events would lead to another sequence. And you could bounce around and your eye would go across and follow the different themes, but it ended up not being about that. It's really about the two extremes, and how things repeat across. . . .

HR: But all good art is hypertext. You know, Basil Bunting asserted that poetry comes from dance and you keep a certain cadence in music, in musical background at least, in the writing. Not necessarily in the voices of the personae in the plays, but in your own sense of composition.

EA: Sure. It's the fact that you can conduct a play when you're directing it.

HR: Right. There's an orchestral shape, there's a form, and you have a sense of completeness when you leave the theater. There's got to have been a form, however unknown to the audience, however separate from the obvious dramatic intentions.

EA: Have you ever been to Mexico City?

HR: Never.

EA: Under Mexico City, under the center of Mexico City, under the main square near the cathedral, they're excavating an Aztec city, and there is a wall of skulls that they're found. It's about twelve feet by ten feet, and it is a wall of skulls.

HR: A representation of a skull rack.

JT: And he thinks I may have gotten the idea for presenting the ovals from that, but I didn't.

EA: But the New Guinea work, when you see that . . .

HR: Yeah, Sepic River work from New Guinea. You get that sense of them.

EA: You do, yeah.

HR: And there's a great value to having that repetition.

EA: And that was a moving experience for you [directed to Jonathan Thomas], seeing that wall.

JT: Oh, it was. It was beautiful.

EA: Whether it related specifically to this stuff or not is hard to say.

HR: And one never does know where it comes out.

EA: Exactly. You're not often sure where you're getting the stuff from. Jonathan wants to have the totems in the show rather than the newer work that he's doing.

JT: You know you were talking earlier of the futurists and all that. That's a big feel of his collection. So, you do have a big interest in Moholy-Nagy and all that.

EA: In the constructionists, yeah, I like that. But then again, I have a lot of African stuff, too.

HR: Which is the wellspring of so much modern sculpture. Maybe all modern sculpture.

HR: Have you ever done visual art yourself?

EA: Not since I was twelve or thirteen.

HR: Did you ever get ideas for pieces looking at other people's?

EA: No. No, I knew I would be imitative and not very good. I mean, I can turn out a perfectly good constructivist wall piece—fake, but okay.

HR: There's something to be said for a highly refined sensibility in any art. It gets carried over. Michelangelo wrote important poetry.

EA: No. It's essential. One of the reasons that I'm happy that I have my Foundation is that it provides working and living space for writers and painters and sculptors; these people get so insulated: sculptors talk to sculptors, writers talk to writers, they're thrown out there in my Foundation all mixed together, and they get to relate to each other, and they learn more about each other's aesthetic. And maybe they start relating more, which is the point.

HR: There are things in each of the arts that can be analogized to the others. There's a core sensibility in each art.

EA: Well, obviously you know a great deal about the theater yourself. What conclusions do you come to from what you look at here?

HR: In this case, I found myself in a really interesting situation. Talking to the curator, and I can only imagine that my job is to bring an art historical veneer to a sensibility. . . .

EA: A rough-hewn sensibility, I trust.

HR: No, not yours. Your sensibility is highly polished. And I'm going to have to pretend that in you there's the professional art historical background and method and mechanism that's lacking, which probably isn't the case. Because most of the time, amateurs, true amateurs, know more than the professionals, since the professionals are obligated to abject themselves to the crap of the profession.

EA: When people do photographs of my loft and of the art in it and stuff like that, they refer to a collection. And I say, no, I'm not a collector, I'm an accumulator. I accumulate stuff that I relate to.

HR: There's a big difference, because a collection has a point.

EA: Yes, and most of them these days are put together by other people, not by the owners.

HR: I've met very few collectors of the recent generation because most of them are really investors who call themselves collectors.

EA: That's right.

HR: You're really a collector, which means you don't have a collection, you have an accumulation.

EA: Yeah, exactly, yes.

HR: And it's the truest expression of affection.

EA: And I'll even have areas where I have a wonderful piece of sculpture up and somebody will say, "Gee, that's really a beautiful piece. Who did that?" And I have to admit that it was part of a railway tie that somebody has put on a stand. It becomes art when that happens to it.

HR: Sure, it is transparent.

EA: And that can stand perfectly well next to anything.

HR: Which says a lot about our time.

EA: Well, I think it says a lot about how things become art. I mean, after all, the African stuff isn't made as art.

HR: Right, which says a lot about our moment in history. Our era is the inheritor of Japanese contextualism and the rough-hewn sensibility of Africa as opposed to the polish of beaux-art with which Africa collided in the early part of the twentieth century—within the fashionable context of Japonisme.

EA: There is something that makes something art, and it doesn't have anything to do with historicism. It doesn't have anything to do with anything except the piece itself is art in context. I remember I saw an exhibit about twenty-five years ago. Beautifully lighted, beautifully hung. They were basically geometric, all slightly different; some of them sort of rough on the edges. And I looked at them for a few minutes and I realized what they were. They were a very, very shrewd collection of manhole covers that had been transformed into art by saying, "Take them out of that context and put them into another context."

You know there's a wonderful thing they have on New York streets that looks like Richard Serra's, great huge rectangular steel plates with a hook thing on the end and maybe a couple of symbols in them? They are such beautiful pieces of sculpture.

HR: But Serra taught us to see that.

EA: No, I'm not sure if it doesn't work both ways. I don't think that we saw them as sculpture only after Serra. I think that maybe we saw them as sculpture because of all art, not just because Serra did similar stuff.

So am I saying to myself, did I think those were art pieces before I saw my first Serra or not? I don't know. It's just as likely that I saw them as art pieces before I saw Serra.

HR: There are fleeting sensibilities that get captured by being contextualized as art, and then we can have a handle on it. That process of thinking has nothing to do with quality, per se, but has to do with the self-consciousness of context, which probably comes out of the occidental experience of Japan in the late nineteenth and early twentieth centuries. And even today there are things that you can talk about as art in Japan that you can't do in the West, because for us art has to be an artifact, a thing made. The Japanese have "moon viewing parties" where the reaction that you're having is the art. It's not the moon; the moon stays up there and is not made by anybody. And when we finally come to that, that the self-consciousness of our aesthetic experience . . .

EA: . . . and context is all.

HR: Yeah. Yes, that could summarize our discussion.

EA: That's the title to your piece: "Context is All." Or mine.

HR: Or yours.

JT: A lot of the things that you have been interested in, you go beyond what is just the object itself, because you're dealing with personalities because you know many people. I mean, would you really collect Milton Avery today?

EA: I saw Milton's work first—before he became terribly famous—and went to his studio. . . .

JT: But maybe you were just educating yourself.

EA: Maybe I was. I ended up with five or six of Milton's paintings. I paid five hundred or six hundred bucks for work out of his studio a long time ago. I like them. I'm not embarrassed at having some Milton Averys, I think they're very beautiful things.

HR: Oddly enough, the very first Milton Avery painting ever sold was to a performing artist. A man named Louis Kaufman, who was a violinist.

JT: I mean, don't you think that, because you're a creative person, and you know a lot of creative persons, that some of what you're interested in comes out of just that process.

EA: It may. I like Matisse a lot, and Milton came out of Matisse. Colorists came out of Matisse, and Mark Rothko's color sense came out of Milton Avery, because Mark admired Milton enormously.

HR: As a matter of fact, Rothko was introduced to Avery by this fellow Louis Kaufman. They had never met before.

EA: Really? How interesting.

JT: We do tease Edward for buying bad examples of people's work, because he does like those odd pieces.

EA: Well, as an example, the only Chagall that I have is a 1908 portrait of his sister reading a book, and it relates to the one in Basel which was painted about three years later. It doesn't have the flying people or even those colors that Chagall got into eventually. It's an early piece and it's a very beautiful painting. And I say: Guess who that is? And nobody knows it's a Chagall. And they say you're kidding. Where are all the kissing people and flying shit? Because I thought he was a very wonderful artist between about 1907 and 1915, a marvelous, serious tough artist. But then he got commercial with it.

HR: That's an interesting case, what happens to people as they soften, because it also happened to Kees Van Dongen and to Raoul Dufy. People forget that, at the turn of the century, Dufy was shoulder to shoulder with Braque. At the cutting edge. But artists come to the precipice, and they look down, and some of them get scared.

EA: One of the oddest histories of famous work is Picabia. I saw a Picabia from about 1918, not very ornate, but in a gold frame, and all it was—you could see right through it to the back wall—there were some vertical, horizontal, and diagonal strings, some of which had been tied together with little cardboard squares, but it was a beautiful, an extraordinary painting, as wonderful as anything that [Marcel] Duchamp did or Joseph Bueys did—two artists that I think are particularly important and that I admire a lot.

HR: And in some ways more difficult, because the precedent for doing less hadn't been there.

EA: Another wonderful artist that nobody pays too much attention to anymore, but of course so much of his work got destroyed in São Pãulo, is Torres-García. You know, his sculpture especially. It's good stuff.

HR: Torres-García is important because he was the one who taught us how to read and look at the same time. Or to alternate or oscillate between reading and looking on the same surface.

EA: But his three-dimensional work, even more than his paintings, his sculpture to me is amazing.

HR: The early Adolph Gottliebs, the "pictographs," come out of that.

EA: Well, his transitional stuff, yeah, is surrealist in the Torres-García manner before he moved into the final stuff. Much better, tougher work. Watching all of those painters work—watching Pollock, watching Mark Rothko—all of them moving through their surrealist thing. . . . It's fascinating.

HR: It was an apprenticeship of attractive emotions.

EA: There was a very interesting exhibit in Houston, Texas, at the Menil in their surrealist collection—a huge surrealist collection—a room there, and I forget what they called the exhibition. It was of things that were accumulated by the surrealist artists, sort of similar to the early African work collected by the cubists. But it was just stuff that surrealists were collecting, an extraordinary assemblage of unlikely things.

HR: Things constellated by affection. Things of affection.

EA: Well, not only affection, I think, but useful. Useful affection.

HR: Artistically useful?

EA: Oh, yeah. Of course.

HR: And is that what your collection is?

EA: I have no idea. My accumulation?

HR: Is it aesthetically accumulated for artistic use?

EA: I can't think in those terms. I find it very difficult to think about myself or my work in the third person. I can't look at it and say what affect does it have or what does it need. I can't do that.

HR: Do you examine the sources of your work?

EA: I know what they are, sure. Some of them that I admire a lot, some that I have a great love for and admire so much. I know where I come from, sure, but I come from so many different sources. I mean, we can start back with the Greeks and work right up to the present. O'Neil's work—when I was a teenager, I saw *A Long Day's Journey into Night,* and *The Iceman Cometh* for the first time when I was sixteen, and it knocked me out. A lot of stuff did. Seeing Tennessee Williams, all those people when I was a teenager, being exposed to the French avant-garde which I was reading before I started seeing the plays, reading Sartre and Camus and all of those people back when I was fifteen or sixteen years old. All that stuff ties in. And, of course, Beckett. But, then again, I don't know what any of it means.

HR: Well, there's also the question: do one's sources ever close off, or as you begin to accumulate experiences?

EA: They shouldn't.

HR: Yes, they shouldn't, but people, as you know, run out of steam.

EA: I see the artists' sources closing off far too often. I think later in the career, even somebody who did as much good work as Diebenkorn did, finally. I said: Okay, he'd hit it, he's hit the good stuff, and he's just going to go on with it. But that happens to a lot of them.

HR: That was attenuated. But you don't know if that's fear or if it's sensible, because unless you really make something your own, unless you kill it so no one else can take it over, it's not yours.

EA: But it's not your own anymore if you're doing it just for commerce.

JT: But some people create their own world and keep enlarging it.

EA: Yeah, but that's insularity, through retreat from the field, because you're not allowing yourself to be open to influence anymore.

HR: And so, while we hope that you're open to influence, the question is really: does the accumulation of affectionate objects, do you think it works on you in some way? Both as a human being and an artist.

EA: Certainly I like to be surrounded by stuff I like to look at. I'm sure it's probably still having some sort of effect, or if it doesn't have any effect anymore, put it in the closet and put something else up.

HR: It's self-curating.

EA: Sure.

HR: We've talked about selecting the objects for this show and your sensibility and historical background behind those choices, and the selection of found objects, but we haven't talked about installation. Because as a curator, what you're going to be doing is mounting these works, and there are different ways to mount things. You can mount them to, as we say, to make a room look harmonious, i.e., decorating. You can make a point historically. You could mount them to illustrate some idea.

EA: This is more—don't put too much in the room—that each piece exhibit itself. You can have a piece that fills the whole wall, and that's fine. Or you can have a small piece this size that needs an entire wall. You have to know how much space each piece needs, and if you're putting two people in the same room, how different do you make them. I don't know how that works as relating or vibrating aesthetic experiences. But I don't like to put too much in a room. I don't know, I'd try to isolate each of these artists from the other.

EA: I wish we had nine rooms here at the Anderson Gallery so I could have one artist in each room. We don't quite have nine rooms, so a couple of them I'm going to have to put together. Put as much space around them as they need.

HR: The idea of space that a work "needs" arises or seems reasonable to us because we see artists as individuals, not part of a choir speaking for society. It's obvious to you, it's obvious to me, but it's something of the moment. Of an extended moment.

EA: So I don't know that there's any governing thing in this accumulation of art. It's just some artists that I think are good and interesting and more people should be paying attention to.

HR: Okay. It's salutary.

EA: I don't have to know artists to like them, to know artists to accumulate them.

HR: And you also have a personal relationship with some of them, you participate in their creative lives, critically.

EA: Mia Westerlund Roosen was doing big concrete pieces on the floor, and I said to her one day: why don't you lean one of them over against the wall? And that changed everything for her. But now, of course, she says: It was inevitable that her work would rise from the floor and be leaning against the wall.

HR: Inevitable as long as you are the instrument of the zeitgeist. And that brings us back to, "would we have known that these steel plates were art if there wasn't a Carl Andre," and chances are we would have had an aesthetic intuition, but it wouldn't have been in the intent of art.

EA: Probably not. But I don't remember having lots of debates with artists, [to Thomas] I try to tell you what to do all the time.

JT: He's notorious for going into studios and saying, "It's done. Leave it."

EA: That's because so many artists keep working on a piece and fuck it up completely. I go to studios and somebody has something that is clearly a finished piece, and it's so busy, so static, because it's finalized. And I see something they're working on, and I just know that if they don't do one more thing it's going to be a more exciting piece. I try to tell them not to do it, not to go any further. Take chances.

HR: Do you tell them to stop painting? "Stop painting that picture." It's the enthusiastic observer.

EA: Well, I'm a busybody. I like to show people what to do. They don't pay any attention to me, anyway.

HR: That's probably because you're articulate. Other people might have intuitions about what they like and not like and not know why. More here, more there. People don't know why they like things and don't like them. Nobody really knows ultimately why they like and don't like things; they can't express their dissatisfactions. They haven't thought about them.

JT: The saddest thing is when people stop working because they physically can't go on, Lee Krasner and people like that who just couldn't do it anymore. They just stopped.

EA: Yeah, because of arthritis. Very sad.

HR: Adolph Gottlieb had a stroke in 1964, and afterward he was able to delegate some of the work to assistants. You can see a difference in the pictures, but because so much of his art had to do with placement and coloring, the mixing of hues and paint, he could give adequate instructions, even from a wheelchair. The pictures could continue. And that's very different from, say, having other people paint your pictures for you. It's a heck of a difference.

EA: Yeah.

HR: And it comes down to what you can offload onto someone else. Lord knows architecture is the best example of that.

EA: Interesting what happened to Henry Moore. He would make this little maquette, and then he would have his assistants make one twice the size and then four times and end up sixteen times the size. The things would normally go from two to four to eight to sixteen. The works looked different as a result.

HR: And when you don't make adjustments for scale—and you can tell this clearly in sculpture—very often pieces suffer dramatically.

EA: I saw something much more interesting, wonderful, about five or six years ago in London. It was an exhibit of Franz Kline's big black and white paintings. Right next to each one of them—which I hadn't known he'd done—was a preliminary drawing.

HR: There wasn't a square inch of improvisation in his pictures.

EA: Startlingly.

HR: He's a great academic or traditional artist, and his paint handling is accurate. People don't understand that about him.

EA: It was startling. I thought that when he worked on every-thing, he did them that way.

HR: You know who's got a wonderful collection of those Kline drawings is Cy Twombly.

EA: Cy Twombly has a collection of them? Now there's a person whose sculpture I admire more than half of his paintings, Cy Twombly. I love his sculpture. They're beautiful things. But that was fascinating to me, Kline, because I thought those were gestural paintings.

HR: He's as spontaneous as Degas. Every inch is planned and laid out. And there are versions of different pictures, and you can see him working on them. When you see the finished pic-tures, you can often see that he's working against gravity. The canvases have been rotated two or three times, which you can tell from the way the paint has dripped.

EA: That doesn't change the experience, because the piece exists on its own terms. But maybe it was a little more exciting when I thought it was all chance, when a lot of chances were being taken with the big brush and the big stuff.

HR: But that raises an interesting question about where the excitement of any kind of work comes from. As you know, Glen Gould gave up performing because he called it "a blood sport." People were sitting around waiting for a wrong note. Why should you have to be on the spot on any given night when you've got the ability to record it? Does that change the nature of the performing art? Well, of course, it does.

EA: The difference between the sound of a live performance and the sound of a recording, of course.

HR: Or the difference between play and film.

EA: Well, no, that's a different difference.

HR: A recording of a performance of a piece of music can be done in a number of takes and edited together. . . .

EA: I know it can.

HR: You're irritated by that?

EA: A little bit, yeah.

HR: Seems inauthentic?

EA: Yeah. I know they do it, of course.

HR: Does that mean that you find improvisation exciting? The risk, the spontaneity, the revelation, confessionally then?

EA: Yes.

HR: Unless it's highly conventional. . . .

EA: It's called rehearsing your ad libs which apparently is what Franz Kline did.

HR: Well, I'm thinking about an art such as Indian classical music, where the melody and rhythms are highly structured so that it is possible to improvise but only within a fairly rigorous system. I'm not sure if you're familiar with this. . . .

EA: Yeah, I know the music. I know where Philip Glass comes from and where he should go back to.

HR: We can erase that comment if you want to.

EA: I don't mind. Keep it in.

HR: Keep it in? It's okay with me. I find such work offensive. I don't understand how anybody gets nourished on that aesthetic.

EA: I don't either.

HR: Particularly when you do, for instance, know Indian music, which is one of the richest artistic traditions in the world, and by virtue of having so rigorously conventionalized what you can and cannot do.

EA: I find Glass pretty offensive.

HR: And that will be interesting, because people looking at the art in this show, who are not conversant with modern art, modernism, may also find the visual minimalism of it insufficiently nourishing.

EA: See, I don't find it particularly minimal, except in the sense that maybe less is more, but it's not minimal in the usual geometric sense.

HR: The art that you've selected I don't find minimal, either. But it may be because it comes informed by a lot of experiences that you bring to it, that I bring to it, that a lot of other people bring to it, and some of that experience is comparative. I know a lot of other examples of it. And some of it is purely the experience of looking, so that you can take smaller and smaller incidents and find them more and more nourishing. But I'm not sure what an uninformed audience will bring to it, and that's what's interesting, because, as you know, there will be some quotient of this audience who will come by virtue of your celebrity. And Lord knows what they're going to make of this. I hope they come out of the show educated and elevated.

EA: I hope so, and I hope some of them will be. My most recent play in Houston has a little nudity in it. And there's one couple—and I'm convinced that it's the same couple who comes back every single night, walks out at the first sight of a breast. One elderly couple—I know it's a different couple each night, but it amuses me to think that it's the same couple who comes back so they can walk out. And there are going to be some people who see this show and say this isn't art. What does it mean?

That's what my adopted mother used to say. She'd come to the house and see a good black-and-white Kandinsky, and she'd say, "What does it mean? I don't know what it means." And I've never understood this comment about art: what does it mean? The same way that no two people see the same play, because no two people bring the same experience, the same intelligence, the same open-mindedness, no two people get the same thing out of a piece of art.

HR: Do you really say with sincerity that you didn't understand her question or that same question when other people ask it?

EA: No, I don't understand the question, because I don't know what is expected and what is asked.

HR: I always thought that people wanted some sort of obvious moral quotient from their art.

EA: Well, they want something recognizable. The more art moves away from realism to abstraction, they get in trouble, these people.

HR: They don't have the same problem with Bach or Beethoven.

EA: Don't confuse the recognizable with the moral. They don't listen to Bach or Beethoven that much. They prefer Tchaikovsky and Puccini. I mean, Puccini is a fine composer. Tchaikovsky wrote some good music, too. But they're not Bach and Beethoven.

HR: So melody takes up the function of a moral component. That's what Stravinsky said: melody is the most artificial thing in music.

EA: And he had some pretty melodic periods, didn't he?

HR: Yeah the Firebird, you can whistle that going down the street.

EA: Well, take Persephone, take a lot of the ballets. Melody,

melody, melody. Of course, he was also using a lot of other people's melodies, too.

HR: And we began this by your confession of your own melodic interest.

EA: Well, I wanted to be a composer. I tell my playwrighting students—I don't teach playwrighting, I have playwrighting workshops at the University of Houston every spring—in theory, at least, you should begin every day listening to a couple of Bach preludes and fugues. It clarifies the mind.

HR: And insinuates a subliminal structure.

EA: Yes, a sense of order. It's always been one of my big arguments about why the National Endowment is hated so much by so many of the know-nothings in Congress, because an aesthetic education allows people to think politically more coherently.

HR: Yeah. Ezra Pound observed that very early on, and if it weren't for his actual politics, he'd be taught in elementary schools in this country. An unfortunate human being and a great artist. It's absolutely true: once your art starts decaying, once you get fuzzy about the art, then rhetoric decays, which means that politicians have a free hand to do whatever they want, because the language no longer means anything. And we've seen that.

EA: Yeah, too much.

HR: The first real deconstructivism came in politics, not in academia.

JT: Why are you so against narrative art, or narrative painting? A lot of people—I mean, a playwright's doing a show, there'll be something about the word.

EA: They're different arts.

JT: No, you really hate narrative painting that has a story.

EA: I don't hate it. I don't relate to it. It doesn't do anything to me for the most part.

JT: People may think that there might be something to do with the spoken word or something in your show that you might curate about art.

EA: Why anybody would *assume* that—since I'm a writer, I'd be interested in art that had words in it? I just find that the ideas in abstraction are so much more fertile and nonlimiting than the ideas in representation.

HR: Particularly at this moment. There will be a time when abstraction will probably be as limiting and exhausted a set of possibilities as doing something as social-realist as *The Oath of the Horatii* today. It will feel leaden, and it will feel associated with a moral-political climate that may be repugnant. I don't foresee it, but it does seem to be one of those historical inevitabilities as the pendulum swings.

EA: Yeah, but I think maybe politically. I mean, look at the way the Soviets reacted against their serious art and destroyed it.

HR: What a disaster. In 1921, they closed the door on modern art.

EA: Yeah, that's right, and Shostakovich at home writing his quartets, sitting quietly.

HR: It's a very small recompense for a tremendous burden of human misery.

EA: Of course.

HR: And also other lost art.

EA: And the poets they killed and all the rest of it. And it was the serious artists who got it in the neck. But I don't hate narrative art. There is some that is very good. I just don't want to spend much time with it.

TONY ROSENTHAL

2003

"DROP BY FOR a minute this afternoon if you're nearby," Halina Rosenthal will say to you on the phone. If you're in New York City, "nearby" means anywhere remotely related to the East Seventies. If you're in the Hamptons, "nearby" means wherever you happen to be in relation to The Springs.

I try to arrange to be "nearby" whenever I can, for Tony and Halina Rosenthal inhabit a special world, and a visit to their oasis refreshes one's spirit splendidly.

One arrives; the conversation picks up from the previous occasion as if time or other matters had not interceded; a bowl of perfect strawberries is all at once at one's shoulder; a platter of crudités or a brie will emerge from nowhere—well, from nowhere but Halina's uncanny realization that these are things you have needed without knowing it.

The "minute" becomes an hour, but that's all right: if they have time for you, you certainly have time for them.

One of the pleasures of the Rosenthals' special environment is that one is surrounded by Tony Rosenthal's work. If you are visiting them in New York City, maquettes and works in progress (and an occasional full-grown giant) can be seen through the contentment and the food. And if you are visiting them in the country, and the weather allows you to be outside—and it always wants to—you can chew on a crisp, sharp radish and look across the green field into the woods, the both with their stand of outdoor Rosenthals.

There are worse ways to spend a "minute."

I became aware of Tony Rosenthal's work long before I began to know the man. Nor was it any of his large pieces in public New York places that drew me to him, though they engrossed me as they appeared. (There are three in permanence now, and one—in Foley Square—that I dearly hope will become fixed, for I have seen it in snow, rain, and sun, and it doesn't falter.)

No, I suspect it was at one of the Whitney Annuals in the early sixties, or at the Kootz Gallery in the same period, that Rosenthal's work began to impinge on my consciousness. It is firmly placed there now, and I can spot a Rosenthal in a second. I can spot a Rosenthal in a second not because the work is all alike, mind you— indeed, the pieces of the past three or four years are of a fascinating diversity—but because each work, no matter its preoccupation, is clearly part of the catalogue of a single, adventurous mind.

(I'm not always so good at this spotting, though. Anthony Caro is a fairly individual sculptor, and I've seen a lot of art in my time, but it is invariable that if I am at a museum and I can't place a piece, it is by Caro. I wonder what my trouble is? You would think that, at the very least, I would be able to make the assumption that a piece I can't place is automatically by Caro, but I don't seem to be able to do even that. I think it is simply that, for reasons having to do with a tiny teenage stroke, or some such thing, the sound "Caro" falls from my mind the moment I require it.)

There is so much good sculpture being done these days! And while I can't speak from the protection of a degree in art history, I dare to say that in the past twenty years sculpture has been easily as interesting and instructive as painting. The line of excellence (or, lines of excellence) running from Pevsner and Gabo and Noguchi and Hepworth and Moore and Nevelson through both the Smiths and Visser and Rosenthal and Serra and—you know who I mean—Caro!—to such youngsters as Trakis, Westerlund, and Duff (this entire list just a skimming of examples), tells us easily as much about the intellectual process of art in the period as an equivalent list of painters would.

It's interesting about sculpture: it lacks the *caché* of painting—how few "superstars" there are in sculpture; maybe because it's heavy and decorators don't relate to it very well. Sculpture proceeds profoundly and quietly, is seldom given to splash, and possesses a quality seldom (though now-and-again) found in painting—it can be both "thing" and comment upon, attitude about, that "thing" simultaneously. Not about the "thing" in context—painting does that all the time if it's any good—but about the "thing" itself, as an absolute.

Enough of this; I'm writing about Rosenthal. The exhibition of his work at Knoedler, early in 1977, was a moment of splendid refraction. In that display, Rosenthal managed simultaneously to crystallize the achievements of his previous years and splay in several new directions. Side by side would be two works of the same sense of size, one forthright and massive, the other subtle and delicate. In one, the steel was stone and had always been where it stood; in the other, the steel was paper and charcoal. In yet another piece, three emblems leaning against a wall became simultaneously a timeless cryptogram and shields placed by giants back from the hunt.

It was an exciting exhibition, and it made me want to penetrate Rosenthal's studio, to see his work in progress and to see how it *did* progress. I was not terribly surprised by the conscientious spontaneity I found, the "size" of the maquettes (a true test), the playfulness, the willingness to try the most unlikely, the least prepossessing. Above all, I think, most impressive was the diversity of one mind, one hand.

As I write this, Rosenthal has been working on the maquette for a gigantic outdoor piece, to be placed in Purchase, New York, at the State University. All by itself it exhibits all the qualities which I find so enriching in Rosenthal's work—solidity, airiness, control, abandon. The completed piece will be sat on, sat in, wandered through, and it will be both "thing" and comment upon, attitude about, itself at the same time.

Also, it will be very much Tony Rosenthal.

UTA HAGEN

2004

Edward Albee delivered this piece at Uta Hagen's memorial at New York City's Majestic Theater *in March.*

WHEN DID I first become aware of the extraordinary Uta Hagen? Was it when I saw her as Desdemona in the electric production of *Othello*, with her then husband, José Ferrer, as Iago, and her then lover, Paul Robeson, as Othello? We all went to that production knowing the scandal—for it was that back then—but Uta wiped it from our minds, made us see without doubt that it was Othello, Iago, and Desdemona up there, and not Paul, José, and Uta.

Could it have been Ugo Betti's *Island of Goats?* I think not, though I will never forget Uta, standing there alone, on a rocky hill, bleating like a lovelorn goat. (I told her once, "You're the best goat I've ever seen onstage!" "Thank you," she said, looking at me oddly.)

Whatever it was leading up to her performance as Martha in my own play, *Who's Afraid of Virginia Woolf?* it eased the beginning of my love affair with her consummate talent. She was tough, highly intelligent, very funny, intolerant of mediocrity, extraordinarily talented and, when the occasion demanded it, heart-catchingly vulnerable.

When it became clear—this was 1962—that my producers, Richard Barr and Clinton Wilder, had lost their minds and were planning to do *Who's Afraid of Virginia Woolf?* on Broadway (chancy decision back then, and maybe even more now—three-plus hours? Broadway?), we all—the producers; my director, Alan Schneider; and I—got together to discuss casting. I confess that our first choice for Martha was not Uta but Geraldine Page—another extraordinary actress whose work had greatly impressed me, as it impressed my cohorts.

Page loved the play and said she would do it. We were delighted, and then the conditions surfaced. Yes, Page would do the role and Lee Strasberg (Strasberg? Who was that?) told Page that it was okay for Alan Schneider to direct the play so long as he—Strasberg—could be there at all times as supervising director, sort of éminence grise. This led Barr, Wilder, Schneider, and me to wonder aloud, "Who the fuck does this Strasberg think he is!?" I told the guys that I didn't much care who the fuck Strasberg thought he was: the demand was preposterous. And, since it appeared that Page tended to do what Strasberg thought she should, out the window went Geraldine and in flew Uta.

I suspect that if we had been able to get rid of you-know-who, Page would have been a memorable Martha, but boy, am I glad we got Uta. She wasn't always easy to work with; she didn't like Alan Schneider much, for example, and I got the impression that her feeling about the rest of us varied between tolerant and further south, but she respected my play and my text, and—at thirty-eight years old—stood on the rocky hill of my play and became a Martha equaled perhaps by only one or two others I have ever seen—including the Martha Uta played at the Majestic Theater in a benefit reading for the HB Studio when she was eighty years old! It was not an elderly actress remembering what she'd done; it was a vital, tough, funny, moving performance by a great actress who some people might have thought was too old for the role. She wasn't. At thirty-eight was she too young to play fifty-two? No. At eighty was she too old? Of course not. She was Uta.

Our paths didn't cross much for several years after *Who's Afraid of Virginia Woolf?* Her husband, Herbert Berghoff, wrote me a letter informing me I was the anti-Christ, perhaps because I had publicly opined that I was unhappy with his performance in Beckett's *Krapp's Last Tape,* because I preferred Beckett's text to what I recall being Berghoff's additions, deletions, and transpositions. But eventually I was allowed to see Uta again, and I was very happy about that. She had a home near mine on the ocean in Montauk, and she would cook for me and a few others. You may add to her Desdemona, her goat, and her Martha, her spinach gnocchi as high points in my theatrical experience.

When I last saw Uta—a few months before she died—she was chair-ridden, clearly very ill and, to my view of it, eager to move on, to close.

Pace.

READ PLAYS?

2004

THE QUESTION IS so absurd that we need not only answer it but find out why it's being asked as well. Most simply put: plays—the good ones, at any rate, the only ones that matter—are literature, and while they are accessible to most people through perform-ance, they are complete experiences without it.

Adjunctively, I was talking to a young conductor the other year whose orchestra was shortly to give the world premiere per-formance of a piece by a young composer whose work I admired. "Oh, I can't wait to hear it!" I said, and the conductor replied, "Well, why *don't* you? Why don't you *read* it?" And he offered to give me the orchestral score—to read and thereby hear. Alas, I do not read music. Music is a language, but it is foreign to me and I cannot translate. If I *did* know how to read music, how-ever, I would be able to hear the piece before it was performed—moreover, in a performance uncolored, uninterpreted by the whims of performance. This is an extreme case, perhaps, for few nonmusicians can read music well enough to hear a score, but it raises provocative issues, including some parallelisms. Succinctly, anyone who knows how to read a play can see and hear a performance of it exactly as the playwright saw and heard it as he wrote it down, without the "help" of actors and director.

Knowing how to read a play—learning how to read one—is not a complex or daunting matter. When you read a novel and the novelist describes a sunset to you, you do not merely read the words; you "see" what the words describe, and when the novelist puts down conversation, you silently "hear" what you read . . . automatically, without thinking about it. Why, then, should it be assumed that a play text presents problems far more difficult for the reader? Beyond the peculiar typesetting particular to a play, the procedures are the same; the acrobatics the mind performs are identical; the results need be no different. I was reading plays— Shakespeare, Chekhov—long before I began writing them; indeed, long before I saw my first serious play in performance. Was seeing these plays in performance a different experience than seeing them through reading them? Of course. Was it a more complete, more fulfilling experience? No, I don't think so.

Naturally, the more I have seen and read plays over the years, the more adept I have become at translating the text into performance as I read. Still, I am convinced that the following is true: no performance can make a great play any better than it is, and most performances are inadequate either in that the minds at work are just not up to the task no matter how sincerely they try, or the stagers are aggressively interested in "interpretation" or "concept" with the result that our experience of the play, as an audience, is limited, is only partial.

Further—and not oddly—performance can make a minor (or terrible) play seem a lot better than it is. Performance can also, of course, make a bad play seem even worse than it is. God help us all! When I am a judge of a playwriting contest I insist that I and the other judges *read* the plays in the contest even (especially!) if we have seen a performance. And how often my insistence results in the following: either "Wow! That play's a lot better than the performance *I* saw!" or "Wow! The director sure made *that* play seem a lot better than it is!"

The problem is further compounded by the kind of theater we have today for the most part—a director's theater, where interpretation, rethinking, cutting, pasting, and even the rewriting of the author's text, often without the author's permission, are considered acceptable behavior. While we playwrights are delighted that our craft and art allows us double access to people interested in theater—through both text and performance—we become upset when that becomes a double-edged sword. I am convinced that in proper performance *all* should vanish—acting, direction, design, *even* writing—and we should be left with the author's intention uncluttered. The killer is the assumption that interpretation is on a level with creation.

I'm not suggesting you should not see plays. There are a lot of swell productions, but keep in mind that production is an opinion, an interpretation, and unless you know the play on the page, the interpretation you're getting is secondhand and may differ significantly from the author's intentions. Of course, *your* reading of a play is *also* an opinion, an interpretation, but there are fewer hands (and minds) in the way of your engagement with the author.

About This Goat

2004

HOW *THE GOAT, or Who is Sylvia?* got to be written is both simple and complex. It is a story of how one play didn't get written and how—in its stead—another did.

Several years ago I discovered that I was thinking about writing a play about intertwined matters—the limits of our tolerance of the behavior of others than ourselves, especially when such behavior ran counter to what we believed to be acceptable social and moral boundaries, and our unwillingness to imagine ourselves behaving in such an unacceptable fashion—in other words our refusal to imagine ourselves subject to circumstances outside our own comfort zones.

I came to the awareness that I was involved in such an adventure not by deciding that's what I wanted to do, but by discovering that that's what I had begun to do—by my awareness of a play constructing itself as an idea, informing me that that's what I intended to write about.

That's the way I work—a kind of unconscious didacticism.

The play forming in my mind dealt with this: a renowned doctor of medicine—happily married, middle aged, at the top of his career—has come to the conclusion that he has reached his limits, is doing nothing but good and is a valued and deeply useful member of society, but that this zenith leaves him feeling incomplete. He feels the need to experience life as many of his patients do—his subjects, if you will—and so (this play was planned during the height of the AIDS epidemic, when even partial solutions were not available) he injects himself with the HIV virus, to suffer as his patients do, thereby to "understand" better the suffering all around him.

The play—had I written it—would have examined the hostility and condemnation this action would have produced, and would have raised questions about tolerable behavior—the effect of his actions on family and friends and—indirectly—the matter of suicide, which is illegal in the United States, and which is what the doctor was, indeed, committing, however slowly.

I mentioned the idea to a number of people whose opinions I respect, and I was shocked by the hostility and condemnation I received for even considering writing about such a matter.

I was surprised, for I thought I was "pushing the envelope" in a way playwrights are supposed to do.

I was completing a play about the sculptor Louise Nevelson, so I put this new idea aside for a while, planning to move it into reality right after. Imagine my surprise, then, when a play opened in a tiny New York City theater with exactly the premise and characters I had been considering.

While the coincidence was staggering, the playwright was someone whose work I knew a little of and he was, as well, a reputable actor. I dismissed anything *but* coincidence from my mind, and decided to see the damned doppelganger. Alas—perhaps—it had immediately closed, having received deploring reviews. Naturally, I quickly decided that it was not the premise that had been at fault, but the execution.

Still—it was a concept I wanted to explore and I put my mind to work. Within a year (all dates approximate here as I do not keep a journal, having decided that since all writers' journals are really intended for publication no matter how private they pretend to be, and since I had not begun one at the age of fourteen or so, when all really revelatory journals begin, there would be no point in beginning later), within a year I had evolved the structure and manner of *The Goat or, Who Is Sylvia?*

I mentioned the idea of the play to a number of people (though fewer this time) whose opinions I respect, and I was shocked by the hostility and condemnation I received for even considering writing about such a matter.

Clearly, I was on to something!—either the collapse of my mind or a set of propositions perplexing enough to demand examination. And on I went.

I showed the completed play to my U.S. producer, a lady wise to the ways of theater, who decided to produce it *on* Broadway (of all places!) in spite of the hostility and condemnation she received from quite a few of her confreres (or, possibly, *because* of it).

The play opened on Broadway in the spring of 2002 and received some very odd reviews, indeed. Aside from hardy and rational souls who were engaged and disturbed, and happy about that, a number of critics behaved as though the author had personally slapped them in the face. (This is, of course, a fantasy most playwrights have enjoyed more than once.) The Victorianism of these responses was amusing but not particularly helpful at the box office.

A few of the more influential daily critics of New York City newspapers "hedged their bets" or—equally hackneyed "did not want to go out on a limb" and wrote reviews making it clear they were hedging their bets, not wanting to go out on a limb. Two of these powerful critics rereviewed the play four months into the run—when the public response had proven to be strong and enthusiastic. One of them discovered that the play had somehow changed and was now far more tolerable, and the other—bless her!—admitted that she'd screwed up royally the first time around and did an honest about-face.

Of course, *some* members of the audience were deeply offended by the play and walked out during the performance. It's kind of thrilling when that happens (and in the United States it's usually with older white couples) but we authors do not intentionally provoke it. We desire to engage, to upset, to trouble, but we want people to stay around till the end—to see if they were right in wanting to leave.

I'm not going to discuss here what *The Goat or, Who is Sylvia?* is about, for I would like you to discover all that for yourselves. You may, of course, have received the misleading information that the play is about bestiality—more con than pro. Well, bestiality is *discussed* during the play (as is flower arranging) but it is a generative matter rather than the "subject." The play is about love, and loss, the limits of our tolerance and who, indeed, we really are.

The play is about what it is about, and all I ask of an audience is that they leave their prejudices in the cloakroom and view the play objectively and later—at home—imagine themselves as being in the predicament the play examines and coming up with useful, if not necessarily comfortable responses.

Considering the quality of the talents involved in this production—actors, director, designers—I am certain that whatever faults you find can be piled up at my door.

Borrowed Time

An Interview with Stephen Bottoms

2005

LET'S BEGIN WITH right now. Are you currently working on any new writing?

Yes, I am. Let's see, the last thing that was done in New York—of new work—was *The Goat,* which is going into rehearsal next month in London, at the Almeida. And I've accepted a commission from the Hartford Stage Company to write a play to go with my play *The Zoo Story.* It's normally an hour long, and I have to keep approving other people's plays, or another one of my own, to be done with it. And it occurred to me that even though I was fairly happy with *The Zoo Story* when I wrote it, I really didn't do a full job on the character of Peter. Jerry we know very well. So I'm writing a play about Peter, before he meets Jerry, called *Homelife.* Peter at home with his wife, Ann, and how this affects his reaction to Jerry—to the extent that it *does.*

So it's kind of a prequel?

Well, I hate the term "prequel," but I suppose I'll be stuck with it. The whole evening I'd like to call *Peter and Jerry-Homelife* and *The Zoo Story*. Anyway, the interesting thing about it is that I wrote *The Zoo Story* about forty-five years ago, which is a long time. (How could I do anything forty-five years ago when I'm only thirty-two now?) But after all those years, I find I'm writing about the character Peter as if it was yesterday. I found I haven't lost contact with him, which is very interesting. At least I don't think I have.

Didn't you once do another piece to go with The Zoo Story, *called* Another Part of the Zoo?

No; not exactly. It was just written for a special occasion—"an occasional piece"—and you know how those are. Even Elgar's were very bad. It was for some friends, for a fund-raiser, but it's not a complete play.

Does it concern you in writing this new piece that people will inevitably compare it with The Zoo Story?

I don't see how they could compare it, unless maybe the writing's gotten better. Some people will try to compare anything, whether they should be compared or not. But I'll be very interested to see how people react to the two of them together. I'll be very interested to see how I react! *Homelife* tells me a good deal more about Peter, and so the balance of what happens in *The Zoo Story* is now more complete.

And would you like them to be performed together in the future?

If I like what happens, I shall *insist* that they be performed together. It becomes a "full evening," as they say. Although I've been to ten-minute Beckett plays that were "full evenings."

Could I ask you about the plays that were first produced last year, The Goat *and* Occupant?

Well, *Occupant* never opened, because our star got sick. It never opened and was never reviewed. It was Anne Bancroft, at the Signature Theater on West Forty-second Street. We got about a week into previews and she got pneumonia, so we never opened. That still has to be done, so I've got to find some time when we can do that.

Could you say a little about what motivated you to write about Louise Nevelson, the sculptor, in that play?

I don't remember. She was a good friend, and I thought she was an interesting dramatic subject.

I'm intrigued, though, by your obvious interest in sculpture. Here we are surrounded by sculptures in your loft.

Yes, a lot of African work, particularly. I keep telling my playwriting students that it's not enough to study literature, you also have to study the visual arts, and classical music, if you want to be a playwright. I started out doing drawings, when I was eight or something, long before I started writing, and I discovered classical music when I was ten or eleven. So I've been involved very deeply with all of those since I was a kid, and I think it's very helpful for a playwright to have a visual sense, and to know music also.

Would you point to any of your plays as being particularly "sculptural"?

Well, of course *Occupant* more than any other. Maybe *Tiny Alice* has some sculptural elements, and a lot of visual elements in it, that a lot of other plays don't have. The mansion with the lights going on and off. It's a very three-dimensional, *object-written* play.

I was reading in Mel Gussow's book that you now aren't sure about Tiny Alice—*that you don't feel you can defend it as you can your other plays.*

No, that's not what I said. It's that it's the one play that I can't recall the experience of having written. I can't re-create the state of mind that made me write it. It's the only one of my plays that I can't, and I don't know what that means. I still like it fine, it's just that I don't recall what I was up to! There was a very nice production of it off-Broadway about three years ago, with Richard Thomas being John Gielgud—in a very different way.

It does seem to be a play that's particularly theatrical in its . . .

Operatic is what you mean, yes. It's a very operatic play: you have to conduct the damn thing. I suspect that I had thoughts of grand opera when I was writing it. I wouldn't be surprised. It's a very baroque and operatic piece.

Especially with that final aria, I guess.

Which I cut, of course. Finally. Sensibly. To about two minutes, from the eleven minutes it was. In a play like that you can have an aria because it's a grand opera, but I also had to cut about half a page from the end of *The Zoo Story,* when Jerry's sitting on the bench with a knife in his gut. In the original version, when I didn't know any better, he had a long, long speech. You can't do that when you have a knife in your aorta! So I cut that, because it was unnecessary. Many years ago. And it made the play a lot better.

Are the plays still published in their original form?

I try to get them corrected whenever they're being republished, especially in acting editions. And there's going to be a new, three-volume edition of all of my plays, through *The Goat* I guess, which will be coming out in the next couple of years. Those will be revised versions. I've cut about five minutes out of *Who's Afraid of Virginia Woolf?* I learn a lot by directing and observing productions. I don't rewrite in the sense of rethinking a play, or contradicting any of the premises in the play. But you know, if I bore myself, I think I'll bore other people, so I cut.

Do you find, when you write, that the work still comes quite fully formed, quite spontaneously?

Yes. Well, that's the illusion we give ourselves. I am doing the writing. But we have to play those games with ourselves that the characters are really alive and talking to us. Because if we don't do that, we don't believe them.

But to what extent do you preconceive a play, what it's going to be about, before you . . .

As little as possible. I hate that term: "what is the play about?" It's about two hours, or thirty minutes, that what it's about. I guess I must know pretty much what I'm going to do, but I really write them to find out why I'm writing them. It's a trick we play with ourselves. I mean there are some writers who plot everything out very carefully—every turn of phrase and turn of plot. I don't do that. I like to find out what I'm thinking about, and surprise myself! If there's no surprise, it's just typing.

I was able once to read the draft manuscripts for Who's Afraid
of Virginia Woolf? *up in the Lincoln Center collection, and I was
intrigued by just how little changed between the first draft and the
final version.*

Yes, there were about six or seven pages at the beginning of Act
Three that I cut, that were unnecessary, and I ended up cutting the
last five minutes of Act Two.

*And is that fairly standard? That you'll make small changes
like that, but nothing more substantial?*

Yes, I think so. I won't rewrite a play, because I'm not the same
person who wrote it. I won't let anybody else rewrite my plays,
so why should I let me? But I will cut or alter a bit of it if I think
that it's become anachronistic or unnecessary. And in *The Zoo
Story* I've had to raise everybody's salary! When I wrote the play,
Peter, a publisher, was earning thirty-seven thousand bucks a year.
Now it's up to a quarter of a million. Stuff like that you have to
change, because the play exists *now* just as well as it would have
in 1958.

You don't feel tied to that time in any way?

No, that's the interesting thing. Most of my plays are not tied
to time, particularly. I can't think of one of them that needs to
be—well, *The Death of Bessie Smith,* of course. That's 1937 and
set in Memphis. But beyond that I can't think of any of them
that need to be tied to a time. *Virginia Woolf,* clearly, is taking
place in the sixties, because there's references to a number of
events in the thirties and forties. But I don't even like there to be
a note—"1962"—or anything like that. You should just let it
float.

Is that because you see the plays as timeless, in some way?

I'm not going to use that phrase, but I don't think they are beholden to specific dates. They're not historical plays, they're not costume plays. I'm always deeply troubled when I'm talking to a costume designer who wants to figure out the way people dressed in 1962. It's ridiculous! And besides, these people are in college, and they always dress the same way. They're not fashion victims. They wear wool and cotton, rather than synthetic fabrics—that's the only thing I insist upon, for a very wise reason. Onstage, synthetic fabrics take the stage lights differently, and they don't look real. Isn't that interesting?

Again, a kind of sculptured concern, in a way.

Yes. And it's a dance concern too, because you've got choreography going on. It's the only art form that's got all that stuff in it.

Coming back to that, I was intrigued by this catalogue from the "Idea to Matter" sculpture exhibit that you curated a few years ago, and by the statement that you have at the beginning of it: "The illusion versus the real"—which immediately seems a very Albee-esque heading—"this represents the fundamental difference between painting and sculpture. In painting, all is illusion: color, shape, perspective. Nothing is real beyond the illusion of reality created by the painter. It is, after all, all flat, all false, and, in the best hands, all wonderful, all real. In sculpture, everything is real: object, color, shape, perspective, and, in the best hands, all is wonderful and filled with illusion. I think that's such a wonderful paradox. Do you have a sense of where theater would fit into that scheme?

Theater is absolute artifice. Total artifice. I mean, the curtain rises and there are a bunch of painted sets, and people—actors—pretending to be characters. And we must have our complete "suspension of disbelief." It is *all* artifice, absolute artifice. But if it works, it becomes more real than anything.

You seem to have been emphasizing that sense of almost self-conscious theatricality more and more over recent plays . . .

Well, once you've experienced Pirandello, a lot of stuff opens up to you. You become aware of a lot more. I think half of my plays—what have I got, twenty-seven plays now?—in around half of them, the fourth-wall concept is broken, and the characters talk to the audience. So I've been doing that for a long time, ever since *The American Dream*. You see, I don't think that it's enough for the audience to be "at the peephole," so to speak—you know, "the spy in the house of love" (or hate). I think the audience needs to be *involved*. And I've learned this from a lot of playwrights—you know, Pirandello, and Brecht—over a lot of years.

When did you first encounter Pirandello?

Many years ago. Reading, I think, because he doesn't get a lot of productions in this country. Is he done a lot in Britain? I don't think so. But he's one of those playwrights who—the plays aren't as *good*, or as important, as his theoretical ideas.

And they don't translate very well.

No, they don't. But then again, they tell us Ibsen doesn't either. They even tell us that Ibsen had a sense of humor. Can you imagine that! I haven't found it in *any* English adaptation of him. But most people who translate him into English don't speak Norwegian.

Maybe the Norwegians have a particular sense of irony that doesn't translate.

They have a sense of irony. But have you been to Norway? I don't see a great deal of laughter echoing off the cliffs.

It does seem, though, that in the past couple of decades, it's almost becoming the norm rather than the exception that your characters will address the audience.

Well, in *The Goat* they don't. In *Homelife* they don't. But it happened in *The Play About the Baby*, it happened in *Three Tall Women*. I won't go back into the dark ages before that. So maybe it's happening every other time, but it always has. I think in half the plays, the fourth wall is broken.

My own contribution to this book is on Lolita *and* The Man Who Had Three Arms, *which I find fascinating plays, in the way they . . .*

I do too. I think we're going to get a production of *The Man Who Had Three Arms* again some time soon. Which version of *Lolita* did you read, the published one?

The Dramatists Play Service version.

Okay, that's basically the version of the atrocity that was produced on Broadway. I wrote a two-evening version, which has never been done, which is the proper version. I admire that book so much, I admire Nabokov so much, and I was shocked by what happened to my play. I'll get sued if I get into it, but it was a combination of a producer that I thought was a criminal, a director who was scared to death of the star, and an actor who to my mind thought he was a much better actor than he was—kept making cuts and changes without my permission. It was an awful experience. I don't know why I didn't just close the whole thing down. Maybe I didn't want to throw everybody out of a job.

But you haven't done any adaptations since then . . .
No, that was the last one. That sort of finished me for a while.

How do you feel about that process of adaptation? Is it something you do to push yourself in different directions?
Well, one of them is not really an adaptation. *Everything in the Garden* is a translation really, from English to American. The nicest part of that for me was taking the character, Mrs. Toothe in the American version, and making her British. In Giles Cooper's version she's a rather unpleasant Jewish refugee, which seems part of that particularly British form of anti-Semitism that I've always disliked—so I thought it would be very proper to have the whore mistress being a very elegant British lady. And that was the major part of the adaptation. Of the others, *The Ballad of the Sad Café* struck me as a highly visual experience, and it worked very well onstage. Only James Purdy and I seem to like my adaptation of *Malcolm*, but I've seen very good productions of that in colleges and other places. And *Lolita* was a disaster, but eventually it will probably be done in my two-evening version, and I think it will be all right then—if we ever get it onstage. I've seen a couple of productions of *The Man Who Had Three Arms*, which was *loved* in Chicago, before it came to New York. And the audience had a wonderful time during the two weeks of previews in New York: they were standing up cheering, and laughing all through it, and then these motherfuckers got at it . . . I rewrote the ending just a little bit, in time for the New

York production, but they wouldn't put it in, even though I was directing it. You know, the part where he grows the foot out of his back at the end, which is much funnier.

What happened originally?

That didn't happen. He was just railing against fate. But I don't understand how anybody thought—how critics decided—that that play was about my career. Because I say, right in the middle of the play, "I didn't write fifteen string quartets, for Christ's sake, I didn't split the atom. I grew a fucking third arm. Where's the talent in that?" How they would pretend it was about me, and that I'd lost my writing ability, is just *gratuitous*.

And why would anybody think that about themselves? And then write about it!

Of course. Totally gratuitous and mean-spirited. But then you learn, very early in your career, that not only is life not fair, life is a lot fairer than theater.

Himself seems to be as much an American Everyman figure as anything.

Yes. And the play is as much as anything an examination of how we construct false idols. And then when we don't like them anymore, we knock them down, and blame them, rather than us.

In that sense, then, maybe it did find its right audience—if it upset people that much, maybe that's what it was for!

Yes, but the audience it found seemed capable of closing it. Which is not a good thing. But we'll get it on.

Was part of the problem there because it played on Broadway, rather than in an off-broadway house? Does that set up particular problems?

Well, there is the double standard of criticism between Broadway and the serious theater. And some things are more tolerated if they're not going to rock the boat. They're going to be seen by fewer people off-Broadway, and are not going to be considered as important—even though the best plays are done there, usually. So there's a double standard, but no, it should have been done right where it was. Liz McCann, my producer since Richard Barr died, she was told, "Shouldn't you do *The Goat* off-Broadway?" She said, "No, these people deserve it!"

It's great that The Goat *put you back on Broadway with a new play, after all this time. You do seem to have felt, throughout your career, that for all its flaws Broadway is the place that should be aimed for.*

The only thing that's important about Broadway is that that's where people take their cues as to what's important in the theater. It has to be *on Broadway.* "If it isn't happening in New York, and it isn't happening on Broadway, then it doesn't matter." It's a preposterous notion. Actually I'm much happier off-Broadway, because all our Broadway theatres are too big, and the pressures are preposterous and other than they should be. I'd much rather have my plays done in a three-hundred-seat theater. But you need to challenge things every once in awhile.

Were you at all concerned at how The Goat *would be received? It seems to have gone down very well.*

Well, yes. A lot of critics came back to see it a second time, when we changed the cast, and they seemed to think it was a much better play. Maybe they should have seen it twice before they reviewed it!

Did you think it changed at all with the second cast?

No, not really. Both casts were splendid. They both did the play slightly differently, but same lines, same intention, same result. No, no cast was better than the other. And I always knew the play was funny and outrageous—and sad, of course—all at the same time. All actors of mine when they're in a play of mine are startled when they first go onstage, in front of an audience, and discover that the play is fairly funny. I remember when Jessica Tandy came backstage after the first act of the first performance of *A Delicate Balance*—the original production—and she was *quivering*. She said, "Edward, they're laughing out there!" I said, "Yes, because it's funny. Get back onstage."

And yet A Delicate Balance *is never talked about as a funny play. Most of the criticism treats it as this very somber piece.*

Well, it is, but it's also funny. I hate any play that's humorless. Which is why—poor Ibsen—I prefer Chekhov to Ibsen.

The Goat really does seem to run the gamut back and forth between total hilarity and quite gut-churning dramatic moments.

I like to catch people like that. I like catching people in the middle of a laugh, and them realizing that it's not funny—or catching them in the middle of something awful, and realizing that you can laugh at it. I like doing that, I guess—since I do it so much.

I was intrigued by your subtitle for The Goat, *"Notes Toward a Definition of Tragedy."*

A definition. Not *the* definition, or a redefinition. "Notes Toward a Definition of Tragedy." This is a paraphrase of somebody's famous book—"Notes Toward a Something Something"— I can't remember who wrote it. Some turn-of-the-century philosopher or scholar.

And is there a particular logic behind it being there, or is it more of a provocation?

Well, it's a fact. So that's why it's there. It's not part of the title—it's a parenthetical comment, which is why it's in parenthesis. The title is *The Goat,* or *Who Is Sylvia?*

But there is that sense in the play—and it's true of The Play About the Baby *too to some extent—that there's this almost Greek-tragic sense of unavoidable* harm *that's going to happen, and there's nothing you can do to avoid it. Is that part of the thinking there?*

Maybe. See, I don't think about my plays very much. I don't think about me in the third person at all, and I don't think about my plays after I finish them, except making sure that everything happens the way I want it to. But I don't think about what they *mean,* or the implications or anything.

As you said, you don't like to talk about what they're "about." Let me ask you instead about Our Town, *which is not one of your plays at all, but which I'm directing right now, back home in Glasgow, and which I understand you're very fond of.*

Well, it's one of my favorite plays, because it is *not* the

Christmas card that everybody thinks it is. It's a real tough play—tough and bitter and deeply moving, but everybody performs it like it was a fucking Christmas card. It's disgusting, most productions you see of it. A friend of mine has been commissioned to make an opera of it, and I wrote him a letter saying that this *does not need* to be an opera. And if you're going to do this opera version of it, pay close attention to what they tell doctors all the time: *do no harm.* It's a beautiful and sad, deeply cold play. Don't you think?

Yes—and very funny as well.
Of course it is.

And I was struck, in working on Wilder, and at the same time rereading all your plays for this book, by a certain shared sense of the need for people to wake up to the world, to live every moment more consciously, I guess. We talked about Pirandello, but is Wilder a particular inspiration for you too?

Well, he has two very good plays—*The Skin of Our Teeth* less so than *Our Town*—but every now and then Wilder has a moment in a play of his that just knocks me out. In *The Skin of Our Teeth*, the one moment where I just burst into tears, almost as soon as I start to think about it, is during the great storm, when Mrs. Antrobus can't find her son, and for the first time we hear his name, as she calls out: "Cain!" That is so chilling and so wonderful. And there's a moment in *Our Town* when Emily comes back from the dead, and she hears her father offstage coming down the stairs, saying, "Where's my girl? Where's my birthday girl?" . . . I'm practically breaking up now . . . It is so moving, and so beautiful. And it takes a particular kind of genius to be able to do that sort of thing. Yet Wilder himself was a kind of cold guy. Did you know that he spent the last ten years of his life writing a book about *Finnegans Wake*? And he never finished it, but he used to send me chapters of it to read, and I could never confess to him that I hadn't read *Finnegans Wake*! But I think those moments, in those plays—well, they obviously had a profound effect on me. And you try to attain that particular kind of magic.

And those moments both revolve around parent-child relation-ships, which is a recurring thing in your work as well, of course.
Yes, that does seem to turn up, but I don't think that's the reason. I think it has to do more with *loss,* or to do with lost opportunity. But it all ties together. Did you notice, Mel Gussow finishes his book talking about Samuel Barber's setting of the James Agee thing, *Knoxville: Summer 1915*? Have you ever heard that?

This is the thing about "One is my mother who is good to me. One is my father who is good to me"?
You should listen to the recording some time—beautiful piece. And so, yes, it all ties together, probably. But I don't think about it very much.

It intrigues me, in that book, that Mel Gussow seems deter-mined to read you work through your biography, and yet at the same time he acknowledges that you have a problem with that.
Well, it does tend to suggest that writers don't have any creative imagination. That we're limited to what has happened to us. You see, I don't think I've ever written about me. I'm not a character in any of my plays, except that boy, that silent boy that turns up in *Three Tall Women*. But that can't be me, since I talk all the

time. No, I don't want to write about me. Of course, I write through my own experiences, and what I write is limited by my ability to . . . *perceive* things. But all biographers do this. They feel it's their responsibility to find the connective tissue, which may be valid, but if the work doesn't transcend the experience that produced it, then it's not worth the trouble in the first place.

How does that relate to something like Three Tall Women, *which is so clearly based on your mother. Is that also trying to transcend those particulars, in a way?*

Well, I had the strange experience when I was writing that play, that I wasn't writing about my adoptive mother—that I was inventing a character. And though there's a lot of fact in there, I did feel I was inventing her. People tell me I made her somewhat nicer than she was. Of course, that wasn't my intention, but it wasn't a revenge piece either. I tried to be very, very objective.

It is very frank, in that she's so obviously so cantankerous and bigoted, and yet it does seem to be a very loving portrait as well.

I had a rather grudging admiration for her survivability. We never got along, ever, and I used to think it was all her fault. But I think I was probably not a very easy kid, and I don't think it was any willfulness on her part to be awful. I just don't think she knew how to be a parent.

Mel Gussow describes how you once stood in for the actor playing the boy during a rehearsal for Three Tall Women.

Yes, and I got so interested in the other people onstage that I forgot my cue. It was only a visual cue, but I forgot it completely. I used to act when I was at school and college—I loved being onstage, but I don't think I forgot my cues back then. It was a very odd experience, playing somebody who's supposed to be you . . . Never mind.

Can I ask you about another of the recurring things in your plays, which is married couples—particularly couples who've been together for a very long time. On one level, they always seem to be at each other's throats, and yet on another level, there seem to be reasons why these couples are still together.

Well, you know, I can't imagine anybody writing a play that would be very interesting about a couple of people getting along terribly well. That would be pretty boring. It's called television. Plays are meant to have dramatic conflict, and if people aren't in conflict, what's the point of writing them? But you do write them hoping that people will stop behaving that way. And in *Who's Afraid of Virginia Woolf?* George and Martha do love each other very much—they're trying to fix a greatly damaged marriage, yes.

What about Marriage Play—*which seems even harder, in a sense, and yet is very playful too?*

I like that play a lot. It's about that awful thing that—eventually you realize no matter how good something is, it's not enough. That you're going to miss out on something. Terrible feeling, and a very important one. It's that feeling that you're going to be settling in, and that you've had all the experiences you're going to have. You know, you have a relationship going on for many years, and you're very happy, but there's a nagging feeling—have I missed the boat somewhere? Is there not something else that would have been better? And that whole play's about that?

So, that's about loss as well, in a way.

Well, can you have lost something that you never had? Yes. I guess you can. So it's about that, basically—but they're perfectly happy together, they enjoy each other. She knows what he's going through, and she's probably going through it herself, but he feels he has to act on it, which is the dramatic problem of the play.

I get the sense that they go through this whole routine quite often.

Oh, I think it's the first time they've been through that one. I don't think it's happened before.

But there is that very Waiting for Godot *ending, where he's saying he's leaving and then he doesn't.*

An homage to Beckett? Not necessarily. It is quite true, but it's not the same thing. "I can't go on; I'll go on." "I'm leaving; I *am*." Yes, but she knows he's not.

These plays that deal with marriage, are they about marriage in the heterosexual sense—or rather the institutional sense—or are they about long-term relationships of any sort?

I don't notice very much difference. I mean, I've been in a relationship for thirty-three years myself, and that strikes me as being as valid, as three-dimensional, as intense as any heterosexual relationship would be.

Have you ever been tempted to write about a same-sex relationship?

Is that a dramatic subject?

Why not?

Maybe I will someday. After the bombing of he World Trade center, we were all asked to write about our reaction to that—they wanted some kind of knee-jerk response. I was here, I saw the plane hit the second building . . . people falling out. I saw the whole thing, so maybe it'll turn up in a play someday. But no, I don't see that much difference between heterosexual and homosexual relationships, if they are two people really involved with each other, trying to make a life together. I don't see that much difference, except that the homosexual couple have to fight a lot of prejudices, and illegalities.

It does seem that The Goat *is a play that takes on questions of sexuality very directly—not in some simple straight or gay way, but in asking people to acknowledge that sexuality is much more complex than people give it credit for.*

Sure. That play isn't about goat-fucking. What I wanted people to do is not just sit there being judges of the characters. I wanted people to go to that play, and imagine themselves in the situation, and really think hard about how they would respond if it was happening to them. That's really what I'm after. Put yourself there. "How the fuck would I react? Why am I making this judgment about those people? Because I probably wouldn't make it if it was happening to me."

And yet, it's a fairly extreme thing to ask people to imagine themselves into.

Really? I know people in this country . . . even Republicans! I mean that's a far more preposterous concept.

Republicans?

Yes.

Well, okay, let's talk about Republicans. I mean, you mentioned 9/11—can I ask you how you feel about the situation right now, here in the States, and with the violence continuing in Iraq? It's off the subject of your plays, but I wonder if it does link up.

I find the erosions of our civil liberties deeply disturbing. I find that the lies that our government tells us are more naked than ever. I find that the attempts on the part of the administration to move us way, way back and away from all the important socio-economic changes we've made over the past forty years are dangerous and disgraceful. And what's more dangerous is the fact that most people don't seem to give a fuck. I find that desperately threatening, so I shoot my mouth off all the time about it. Which it's my responsibility to do. How much faith have you lost in Mr. Blair?

Just about all of it.

I would think so. I think he's lying too, about so many things. I mean, there was no excuse—maybe there was a *reason* for going into that war, but all of the *excuses* we were given were clearly fallacious. They were just lying through their teeth and knowing it. And that's greatly troubling to me.

You've always had this activist streak, in terms of your work with PEN, and your tendency to get up and make speeches about these things. Do you think these political concerns come through in your playwriting?

I just have the feeling that the more we are in contact with ourselves, and *think*—spend some time thinking, rather than just in knee-jerk reactions to things—the more we'll vote intelligently. And so all plays are political, way deep down underneath.

Your plays always seem to involve lies or power games on one level or another . . .

And also, to a large extent, a number of them—like *A Delicate Balance*—are about people who have retreated from activism of any kind, and are living the rest of their lives on the surface. And I'm deeply opposed to that too.

So there's a level of affirmation that's going on, in terms of wanting to push people back out there?

That's right, yes.

I'm reminded of Peter Brook's comment about Samuel Beckett— that his "no" was so insistent that it became a kind of a "yes."

Well, you know what Sam said when somebody asked him why he kept on writing all these pessimistic plays? "If I were a pessimist, I wouldn't write plays." He made the assumption that there was communication possible. We all make that assumption when we write something. A whole set of assumptions: (a) that we have something to say, (b) that we have the ability to say it, and (c) that somebody will listen. Now, it could break down anywhere, but we make the assumption, because we are trying to change people's perceptions. That's what art is about—all art.

You seem to share with Beckett a very bleak streak—yet there's also this more positive, affirmative side to your writing.

The way we are, and the way we could be. They're two different things.

And do you have faith in people's ability to change?
The ability, yes. The willingness, no.

I like, for example, the end of Seascape, *with that line:*
"Begin."
It's a threat. It's really a threat. So many productions of
Seascape make the lizards cute, but right at the end there, they're
going back under the water and destroying evolution—which
amused me a lot. They're going back under the water because
it's too awful up here, and they're learning things like loss and
crying and death, which they'd never known. So they're wanting
to go back home, even though they can't. And Charlie and
Nancy say, "No, please wait, we can help you." And Leslie turns
around and says, "Okay buddy, begin." Meaning, "and if you
don't succeed, I'll rip you to pieces." That's the whole intention
of that last line. If you misunderstand that, then it's a misunderstanding of the play as profound as many misunderstandings of
Our Town.

So is Seascape *comparable with* A Delicate Balance *in that*
sense? That the threat to go back under the sea is like the threat
to withdraw into yourself and away from the world?
Well no, it's different, because they *can't* go back under. Evolution cannot be denied—except by the religious right in this
country. It can't be denied: they want to, but they can't, so they
are going to have to evolve. And they *are* going to have to put up
with the self-awareness of death and loss and all the rest of it. So
it's not the same thing.

I suppose also that one is a more realistic play than the other.

Oh, I think that *Seascape*'s absolutely realistic. I directed the first production of that, and I remember I had to tell my actors who played the lizards, "You are not metaphorical, you are real creatures!"

Who happened to speak perfect English.

Because we're doing the play in America. It occurred to me it would have been funny—and I almost did it—to have them coming up speaking French. They thought they'd landed on the French coast. It seemed to private a joke to do, but if they come up on the French coast, then obviously they're speaking French. These are things we take for granted.

Seascape *also seems to me to typify your use of a certain sense of wit and charm. Maybe this is just my perception, but that seems to have become more and more a part of your work over the past twenty years or so.*

It was there in *Virginia Woolf*, except that everybody thought the play was so shocking that they didn't see it. I don't think the work has changed very much. I mean, there was an awful lot of funny stuff there in *The Zoo Story*. The ending's not very happy, but a good production of that will see the humor in it . . . "*charm*"?!

Do you have a problem with that?

No, I don't, but I don't know quite what you mean.

A certain twinkle in the eye, perhaps.

I've become Father Christmas, have I? I see.

No, but in things like Finding the Sun, *or* Fragments, *people seem to be sitting back a little bit more, and reflecting with a certain . . . dry . . .*

I think it's always been there. But perhaps, as I have evolved, I take myself less seriously. You may be right.

*You also seem to have taken to giving some of your plays generic titles—*Marriage Play *and* The Play About the Baby, *and* Fragments *sort of tells you what it is too.*

Isn't that helpful?

It is. But is that a way of saying, "Untitled," or . . . ?

No. A title is a title. That's the thing with *Marriage Play:* when people are going to do it, they always make the mistake of calling it *The Marriage Play,* but it is both a play about marriage, and it's a play that takes place in marriage. It's a double title. Same way I don't waste names with characters.

I guess The Play About the Baby *works that way too. It happens around this thing that turns out to be an absence.*

A reality first, and then an absence. A real baby that is taken away. That troubled me, that some critics thought it was tied to *Virginia Woolf.* They're totally opposite things. Eventually the young couple realize that they *cannot have* the baby, and therefore it must disappear. For George and Martha it's the opposite.

Certainly the London critics seemed preoccupied with that link. But it was interesting that The Play About the Baby *didn't go down so well in London, and then did very well here in New York.*

Yes, I don't know why. The play was very much the same. There were no textual changes.

Do you think that the way a play is directed can substantially change the way it is perceived, given that the text is more or less fixed? When you chose to direct Virginia Woolf *in 1976, you said then that you were trying to amend certain misunderstandings about the play.*

Well, I thought the play was a lot funnier than it was in the original production. I didn't change anything, merely *revealed* a few things . . . I didn't think the production of *The Play About the Baby* in London was all that bad. There were a couple of problems, but I don't know quite what went wrong. Lord knows, the actors were fine. Anything Frankie de la Tour is in is good. Axiomatically.

Is she one of your favorite actors?

Yes, I love her. But there are a lot of actors and actresses that I seem to have worked with with some frequency over the years. I was very happy in London working with Peggy Ashcroft, and I like working with Frankie; I've worked with Maggie [Smith] well. Here, you know, there was Colleen Dewhurst, and Irene Worth, people like that I've had good relationships with. And [Elaine] Stritch, who actually played Martha in *Virginia Woolf* when she was thirty-something. Yes, some actors I seem to work very conveniently with.

Do you find there's a particular reason for that? Are they not imposing certain things, or bringing certain things to bear?

Well, classical training I find very important in an actor. Someone who really keeps working onstage, and doesn't just come in every now and then from a TV show, and *deign* to do a play. And there's intelligence—real intelligence, as well as an actor's intelligence—and the ability to handle language. Some of my plays are fairly baroque in language. Those are all important things.

And yet John Gielgud, in retrospect, was perhaps not the ideal person for Tiny Alice, *despite his ability with language.*

No, he wasn't. The sexual fires weren't quite right. I mean, his ability with language was extraordinary, but I've seen younger people do it better. He was a little too old for it. But I was grateful to have him.

Do you find that the Method approach to acting can be a hindrance at all—if people are wanting to know why they're doing things, when there may not be a simple, logical motivation?

Well, I don't find that good British actors, for example, have no interest in why they're doing things. I find that the two acting methods, of the very best actors, are quite similar. They know *why* they're doing it. John Gielgud kept saying, all the way through *Tiny Alice,* that he didn't understand what he was doing, but that was bullshit. He understood perfectly well: he was a bright man. And Ralph Richardson, for example, always knew what he was doing. He was as crazy as they come, and his reasons for doing things may have been bizarre, but his three-dimensionality and believability were never in question. It's only with second-rate actors that you can make the joke about the difference between British and American actors. Any actor who's really any good is a three-dimensional actor, and what happened at the [Actors'] Studio wasn't really any different from what was going on with actors who weren't catalogued in that way. I'm not going to believe any actor unless I believe what the character is doing, so I expect the actor to get there by whatever method. Whenever I'm directing a play—mine or Beckett's or anybody else's—I always tell the actors, "I want you to do whatever you want, with the exception that I want you to do the lines, every word that the author wrote, in the sequence that he wrote them. You can do whatever you want, as long as you end up with exactly what the author intended."

Do you still maintain an interest in directing?

I haven't directed in five or six years now, but yes, I'm still interested. But it's a lot of work, and for some odd reason I keep getting busier all the time.

You're certainly showing no signs of retiring. I notice in two or three of your plays that you cite seventy-five years old as the average male life span. Am I right that you're seventy-five now?

Yes. I think I should up that. How about ninety? But one lives on borrowed time anyway. All of us.

We've talked a little bit about some of your predecessors—Beckett, Wilder, Pirandello . . .

And Chekhov. I think the three most important playwrights of the twentieth century are Chekhov, Pirandello, and Beckett. They've had a really profound influence on us. And Irving Berlin, of course.

How about the people who've come after—your protégés, as it were? People like Adrienne Kennedy, John Guare . . .

Well, I don't like to talk about other playwrights besides Samuel

Beckett and Chekhov. There are some very good ones, and you've mentioned a couple who I think are very provocative and interesting, but with people who are working in the theater, I don't think one should have much of an opinion about "their work." One should have an opinion about individual pieces, yes. This play works, that play does not work. But with the possible exception of me, I can't think of any playwright, all of whose work I have some admiration for. And I know that I'm wrong about me. But I don't think that judgments can be fairly made until fifty, seventy-five years later.

My point is that you seem to have maintained—ever since the Playwrights Unit in the sixties, and right through to the work you still do in Houston—a certain concern with mentoring young writers.

I think there's a responsibility for those who know their way around the craft to try to help people that they think are talented. There are two big boxes right there in the front hall with a hundred scripts that I'm supposed to read, in case I go back down to Houston and teach this year. I'm supposed to choose my own students, and I choose the ones that I think are provocative, and can be helped, and haven't made up their own minds about what theater's all about yet. That's a responsibility, to push people in the direction of writing like themselves, and not being *employees.* I tell them to avoid all formulas, to stop imitating, stop copying, because there's enough commercial crap around. And I also try to warn them about the pitfalls of theater—the commercial pitfalls. If you know something, you should share it, right?

I guess they're the new YAMs now, and you're the FAM?
Well, I've turned into one. I rewrote that play a little bit. I changed some of the references to who the young playwrights

were. I took myself out of that category. This was a few years ago. But that play is really just a magazine article. I didn't even think about it as being performed.

Yet it was quite a provocative piece when it was first published. You were seen as off-Broadway's "enfant terrible," or "angry young man," or whatever.

Slogans. We're all supposed to represent something. Being is not enough. We have to be metaphorical.

And what do you represent now?

I don't know. A survivor of some sort.

I guess I'm asking if you're still interested in provoking people, in prodding them a bit.

Well, as I say, if a play is not provocative, in the best sense of the term . . . I mean one shouldn't be aggressive. I don't sit down at my desk and say, "I must now provoke." But it seems to be that it's my determination to shake people up, and make them change in some way. And that's fine. It's called playwriting.